AFTER THE LOCUSTS

How costly forgiveness is restoring
Rwanda's stolen years

Meg Guillebaud

MONARCH
BOOKS

Oxford, UK & Grand Rapids, Michigan, USA

Monarch Books and The Church Mission Society

First published in the UK in 2005 by Monarch Books
(a publishing imprint of Lion Hudson plc),
Mayfield House, 256 Banbury Road, Oxford, OX2 7DH.
Tel: +44 (0) 1865 302750   Fax: +44 (0) 1865 302757
Email: monarch@lionhudson.com
www.lionhudson.com

ISBN-13: 978-1-85424-717-9 (UK)
ISBN-10: 1-85424-717-4 (UK)
ISBN-13: 978-0-8254-6091-3 (USA)
ISBN-10: 0-8254-6091-3 (USA)

Distributed by:
UK: Marston Book Services Ltd, PO Box 269,
Abingdon, Oxon OX14 4YN;
USA: Kregel Publications, PO Box 2607,
Grand Rapids, Michigan 49501.

Unless otherwise stated, Scripture quotations are
taken from the Holy Bible, New King James Version,
© 1979, 1980, 1982 by Thomas Nelson, Inc.
Used by permission. All rights reserved.

British Library Cataloguing Data
A catalogue record for this book is available
from the British Library.

Book design and production for the publishers by Lion Hudson plc.
Printed in Great Britain.

Contents

Glossary

interahamwe	Literally, "those who join together"; the name given to the bands of killers who slaughtered Tutsi with machetes, clubs with nails in them or hoes, often forcing villagers to kill their neighbours
Muzungu (sing)	A white person
Bazungu (pl)	White people
Imbabazi	Mercy or forgiveness
Icyiru	Compensation agreed between two families to ensure reconciliation
Inzigo	The gulf that existed between two families where no compensation could be agreed for a grave offence
Kwatura	To confess publicly
Kwihana	To repent
Muhoro	A small sickle used for harvesting sorghum
RPF	The invading, and eventually successful, army comprised largely of Tutsi refugees from Uganda, together with dissatisfied Hutu who had fled the previous government
Gacaca courts	Traditional courts set up in local areas in an effort to deal with the backlog of prisoners
Longdrop	A pit latrine

AEE	African Evangelistic Enterprise. Team Leader: Antoine Rutayisire
Solace Ministries	Christian organisation primarily concerned with rape victims and widows. Director: John Gakwandi
PHARP	Peace-building, Healing and Reconciliation Programme. Director of Women's Work: Mrs Julienne Kayijuka
MOUCECORE	*Mouvement Chrétien pour l'Evangelisation, le Counselling et la Réconciliation* or The Christian Movement for Evangelism, Counselling and Reconciliation. Director: Michel Kayitaba
NGO	Non-governmental organisation
UNHCR	United Nations High Commission for Refugees

Foreword

In April 1994 the world was stunned by an appalling genocide in Rwanda that left at least 800,000 dead and hundreds of thousands wounded and traumatised. For the most vulnerable, children and old people, the result was abandonment and utter despair. My wife and I paid an official visit to the country a few months after the genocide and were shocked by the situation that greeted us – divided and guilty churches and communities; vengeful and grieving families; distrustful and watchful politicians and community leaders.

It was on that visit that I met again the wonderful Guillebaud family that had given such devoted and loving service to Rwanda. For them, and many Christian leaders in the country entrusted with the gospel of Jesus Christ, despair cannot and should not have the last word. There has to be a better way and the gospel offered it. In Meg's last book *Rwanda:The Land God Forgot?* she narrated the circumstances of the genocide and the conditions that led irrevocably to the breakdown of trust between Hutus and Tutsis. She revealed the fact that the outside world was already aware of the deep unrest in the region; and, even though United Nations troops were in the country at the time, little effort was made by the international community to intervene. It is a shameful and shocking story of neglect by Western powers.

In this, her second book, *After the Locusts*, Meg discusses the underlying issue of how one deals with the human desire for revenge and the understandable feeling that there should be an "eye for an eye and tooth for tooth". She shows that this is a totally inadequate response because it only engenders more violence and hatred. Forgiveness has to have roots and a basis in understanding and goodness if it is to be lasting in its effectiveness. In this moving and honest book, Meg Guillebaud shows, from the suffering and deep grief of Tutsis and Hutus, that the Christian faith alone shows the way divided communities may find hope and healing in genuine forgiveness through the cross of Jesus Christ. Drawing upon the testimony and experience of others, she demonstrates the amazing power of love. As I read the book I thought of other countries beside Rwanda where this story might well be instrumental in creating a culture of understanding and hope: Palestine and Israel, Kashmir and Iraq, as well as relationships between Jews, Christians and Muslims.

In Rwanda green shoots of hope are appearing and in Meg's own words, "God is restoring the locust years." I commend this book wholeheartedly. It is a book for our times.

Lord Carey of Clifton
Archbishop of Canterbury (1991–2002)

Prologue

Panic! Locusts everywhere! A cloud of green raised under foot, and a horrible crunching noise. Despair in faces of people who know that this means famine. The unholy cloud lifts and flies on, leaving only bare ground. Every particle of green has been eaten. There will be no harvest until the next crops are sown.

The prophet Joel used this imagery as an apt description of a marauding army coming to devastate Israel, who had broken their covenant with God and thus forfeited his protection. Through his prophet, the Lord God calls to his people: "'Turn to me with all your heart, with fasting, with weeping, and with mourning.' So rend your heart and not your garments; Return to the Lord your God, for he is gracious and merciful, slow to anger and of great kindness" (Joel 2:12–13).

In 1995, Rwanda in many ways resembled a field after the locusts had left. It was still green with an incongruous beauty, but ugly scars of war were everywhere, and a smell of death. Despair and devastation was visible in every face. Tales of horror poured from every new visitor. The church, too, was thoroughly demoralised after its failure to stand up for the right. Many churches had been scenes of dreadful massacres; many church leaders were in exile, fearful to return and face implication in those terrible events; and their people felt that they had lost the right to speak words of healing and peace in the dreadful aftermath of the genocide.

A few people began to see that they had survived the genocide for a purpose. Michel Kayitaba felt God calling him to a holistic approach, looking to practical needs, while teaching on repentance, forgiveness and reconciliation. John Gakwandi was moved by the plight of widows, many of whom had been raped and were homeless. He heard God calling him to comfort his people. Meanwhile, in Nairobi, Julienne Kayijuka was working among refugees, looking at ways to resolve conflict between Christians of the different ethnic groups who were meeting separately to pray to the same God. Later she moved back to Rwanda and is now running seminars on peace-building and conflict resolution throughout Rwanda. Antoine Rutayisire was asked to restart the work of AEE to help the survivors in practical ways, and to call the nation to repentance. He was joined by Dr Rhiannon Lloyd from Wales who started a remarkable seminar of healing and reconciliation in all the key cities of Rwanda.

As the call to repentance and the message of the loving God who had not deserted his people went out, the first stirring of hope could be seen among his people. They began to believe what Joel had told his people centuries before, that God could restore the years that the locust had eaten. This is not to say that murdered families would be brought back to life, but that God would rebuild his church and could even redeem their pain.

Ten years later, it is hard to recognise in Rwanda the devastated land of 1994. Despite undercurrents of tension and hatred, the country has made a remarkable recovery. The church, too, has made a comeback from those demoralised years. God is restoring the locust years.

Two years ago I was asked to write this book on forgiveness. I had been hearing some incredible stories of people who had forgiven appalling injuries. As I have travelled throughout the country listening to these stories, I have been humbled by their faith and their capacity to forgive. Every story in this book was recounted to me personally or told by someone who was present. When I have occasionally used a different name to protect the identity of the person concerned, I have always indicated it. The others agreed to be identified.

I have referred to four of the many Christian agencies working for healing and reconciliation in Rwanda. Members of each agency have attended seminars run by others and incorporated new teaching into the body of their work, so their teaching is very similar. I have tried to acknowledge where I have received the different strands of teaching, but I trust they will forgive me if I have wrongly assigned what I have learnt. Often it is because I have heard it from several different sources.

I am particularly grateful to Antoine Rutayisire, Dr Rhiannon Lloyd, Anastase Sabamungu and Joseph Nyamutera from African Evangelistic Enterprise; Michel Kayitaba and Marie Goretti from MOUCECORE; Julienne Kayijuka from PHARP and John Gakwandi from Solace Ministries, all of whom have given me much time and encouragement as I attempted to tell the remarkable story of healing in a land which only ten years ago was torn by one of the worst genocides the world has yet seen, as nearly a million Rwandans were killed in 100 days.

I would also like to thank Mrs Jo Fisher, Dr Paula Winsor Sage, Mrs Merle McCulley, Miss Linda Manning, Professor John Guillebaud and Miss Elizabeth Arbuthnot who read my manuscript in its many stages and have made several helpful suggestions, encouraging me to continue when I was ready to give up. All opinions expressed are my own.

I would like to thank the following publishers for granting permission to use extracts from their publications:

- Hodder and Stoughton Limited for use of material from *Our Little Secret* by Tori Dante with Julia Fisher on pp 127–130
- Darton Longman and Todd for use of material from *How to Forgive* by John Monbourquette used frequently through the book; excerpts from *How to Forgive: A Step-by-step Guide* by Jean Monbourquette. 2000, NOVALIS – Saint Paul University, Ottawa, Canada. It is used in this title with permission of the publisher. To order: http///www.novalis.ca or cservice@novalis-inc.ca
- African Enterprise for use of material from *Faith under Fire* by Antoine Rutayisire on pp 34–36 and p 110
- Derek Prince Ministries for use of material by Derek Prince on pp 74–76
- Mercy Ministries, Geneva for use of material throughout the book from *Healing the Wounds of Ethnic Conflict* by Dr Rhiannon Lloyd with Kristine Bresser

May this book begin to transform the Western view of Rwandans as savages; may we be prepared to learn from their story, to the glory of God.

References are to the New King James Version of the Bible except where indicated.

CHAPTER ONE

The need to forgive

"Deliver me, O Lord, from evil men; preserve me
from violent men, who plan evil things in their
heart, and stir up wars continually."

(Psalm 140:1–2, RSV)

"**N**early 100 people are buried here," said
Wilberforce as we stood by a large grave
in Kigali. "We don't know the names of half of them, but I
know that Nora and three of our children, Jean-Claude,
Claudette and Francine are among them. Also the nursemaid
of our youngest, Celine. She chose to die with the family even
though she was Hutu and the killers told her to leave." He
took me to the burnt-out skeleton of a house. "All the Tutsi in
this neighbourhood were pushed in here," he explained. "The
interahamwe were outside and would not let anyone escape,
except that someone took away the little children, including
Celine. Then they set fire to some rubber tyres and pushed
them inside. They choked to death in here. Not one escaped."
He paused and added, "The awful thing is that those who did
it were our neighbours and we knew them well."

Wilberforce, who had been out of the country when the
killing started, showed me the grave where his father, brother
and sister-in-law were buried, together with six other members of the household. They had been shot the day after the
President of Rwanda's plane had been shot down, signalling
the start of the genocide in April 1994. They were moderate
Hutu who might have been expected to object to the slaughter. By a series of miracles, Wilberforce had been reunited

with his young daughter, Celine. His oldest son, John, had been studying in Nairobi.

I had returned to Rwanda, the land of my childhood, in February 1995 and was learning about the fate of several of my friends. As we were returning home at the end of a long day, Wilberforce said, "I know that as a Christian I am meant to forgive – but how? Those who did this are not repentant. Surely, if I forgive them it sets them free to do it again."

Ellen[1] was a Tutsi girl, still living with her parents and trading foodstuffs to earn a living in 1994. She had become a Christian the year before and was growing in her faith in an Anglican church in the extreme south of Rwanda. She was totally unprepared for the savagery of the war. At one point, she was repeatedly raped by members of the local *interahamwe*, and left for dead.

As it became more settled after the war, she tried to resume normal life, going back to trading and pretending to herself, and everyone else, that she had never been violated. Rape is not something that a respectable Rwandan woman would admit to, as it reduces almost to zero her chances of marriage. To her relief, she did not conceive and other possible consequences did not enter her head.

In 1998, she married but soon began to feel ill with chest pains. Her husband was very good to her, caring for her during her six-month stay in hospital. She seemed much better and resumed her duties, digging in the fields and looking after her husband, but to her dismay she could not conceive. For the next few years she was happy, except for that sense of inadequacy about not having a child. She still had occasional bouts of illness, but nothing serious.

Early in 2002, to her great delight, she found that she was pregnant. When she went for a check-up, the hospital recommended that she be tested for HIV/AIDS. She was devastated to find that she tested positive as did her husband. She was told that in order to protect her child she could not breast-feed, a serious problem because of the expense of finding sub-stitute milk. She still lived in the community where she was raped and saw those who raped her walking around the town.

How could the church help her to come to terms with the fact that not only was she ill, but that she had given the disease to her husband whom she loved? How could she face seeing almost daily the ones who had violated her? What was she going to do for her beautiful daughter who would probably grow up an orphan? Is it possible to forgive in such circumstances?

The church had started a group for AIDS victims. It is a co-operative without any resources, but they visit each other, comfort and encourage each other. They are open to anyone from any faith or none. The only criterion is that they have AIDS. Ellen calls them her lifeline. She said, "I know how much God has forgiven me. I cried out for his help in the war and he did help in many ways. How can I not forgive those who harmed me?"

Edward,[2] a Hutu, was imprisoned when he and his family came back from Congo. He had not been involved in any killing but a neighbour coveted his fields and accused him of involvement in the genocide. His wife had to fight for her rights. She visited him in prison, taking him food every week, food she could scarcely spare from their two children. She was not a widow but she lived like one. Year after year, this difficult life continued until finally she gave in to the blandishments of one of her neighbours and consented to live with him as his second wife. Edward wondered what was happening when she stopped visiting him, and he barely survived on handouts from others. Eventually, he was declared innocent by the courts and released. He said, "Although I have become a Christian in prison and can thank God for that, I'm filled with fear for the future. I don't know how I'm to live. My wife has another child by the man who has taken over my house and my fields."

How can he forgive those who falsely accused him, his neighbour who has stolen his wife or his wife for abandoning him? And what of her complicated emotions? How can she come to terms with the lost years? Can God restore them? For years she has been living an unnatural life, struggling to make ends meet, visiting a man who had become a stranger to her, taking food from her children to give to him. Why should she not gain something from a life which has become too hard? How can the church help in a situation like this? What have Christian love and forgiveness to say to these lives?

Rwanda is filled with such stories. Hardly a soul exists who has not lost members of his family, a limb, or his home. It is a country where the scars of war and genocide go very deep. Reconciliation is talked about, but the true implication comes home when a man is released from prison and comes back to live in the community where he killed neighbours. How can reconciliation happen? Is forgiveness possible? Why is it important? And having forgiven once, why do the feelings of anger or shame keep on returning? Indeed, how is it possible to forgive at all?

Few of us can forget the scenes of savagery and horror that filled our television screens in 1994, but not many understand what led up to it. In many cases it was shown as another cycle of the ethnic violence erupting after centuries of hatred and repeated violence. The truth is much more complicated than that. The story is told more fully elsewhere.[3] What follows is a description of a few of the key events which led to the massacres of 1994.

Rwanda is a small, landlocked country in the centre of Africa, a few miles south of the equator. It is the most densely populated country in Africa, about the size of Wales (26,340 sq km), with a population of about 8 million and a population density of 290 per sq km. It is a beautiful country, known as the Land of a Thousand Hills or the Switzerland of Africa.

The root of the recent problems in Rwanda is the animosity between Hutu and Tutsi, with both ethnic groups despising the Twa who are pygmoid. These ethnic groups are not true tribes as elsewhere in Africa, since they share the same culture and speak the same language. Rather they could be divided into social classes: Tutsi cattle-herders, Hutu cultivators and Twa hunters and potters. The king was the mystical leader, almost magically identified with Rwanda, from whom the people received their direction for life. Before the Europeans came, there was much intermarrying and movement between the first two groups, though the Twa tended to be despised by the others as "non-people". Any Hutu, or indeed Twa, who became wealthy or who rendered a special service to the king could be "tutsified" and would be given a Tutsi wife. In the north independent Hutu princedoms failed to acknowledge the supreme authority of the king.

With the coming of the Europeans, first the Germans in 1897, followed by the Belgians in 1919, the relatively stable society changed, and many Rwandans blame the *bazungu* or whites for the problems of their land. The Germans found it administratively easier to rule through the king and his chiefs, and they insisted that the independent Hutu princedoms be incorporated into the Tutsi monarchy. In 1912 there was open revolt in the Hutu princedoms of the Ruhengeri and Byumba areas which was defeated by the king with the assistance of the Germans. Many Hutu were slaughtered and were forced into submission to the king. As a result they despised the Hutu of the south who had voluntarily submitted to Tutsi domination.

When the Belgians started to administer Rwanda under a League of Nations mandate, they continued to rule through the monarchy and their chiefs. In 1933, they ordered a census in the country, issuing identity cards to everyone which fixed their ethnic identity. Anyone who owned more than ten cows was regarded as Tutsi. Thereafter their ethnicity followed the father's line and there could be no further movement between the groups.

The chiefs were Tutsi and often ruled with arrogance, some with cruelty; and the many poor Tutsi began to feel themselves superior to their Hutu neighbours. The seeds of ethnic violence were sown; the locusts were beginning to gather. In the 1950s there was a change of heart in the attitude of Belgium towards the Tutsi, and they began supporting the Hutu. In 1959, there was a violent revolution and the Tutsi were overthrown in an attempted genocide. Many fled to surrounding countries or were relocated in an inhospitable area called Bugesera around Nyamata, where some of the worst massacres happened 45 years later in 1994. Successive waves of slaughter took place over the next few years, particularly in 1964 and 1973.

A *coup d'état* in 1973 brought in President Habyarimana, and the killing stopped for the moment, but over the following years, in many ways, the Tutsi were made to feel inferior. Depending on the areas where they lived and the attitudes of the political leaders, many found it impossible to get an education or to hold down good jobs except in the private sector. Despite this, many succeeded and life appeared to be normal for many years.

In 1990, Tutsi refugees who had grown up in Uganda but had been denied full citizenship there, together with a number of dissatisfied Hutu, invaded Rwanda from the north. Fears that a return to Tutsi rule would bring renewed submission to them, even amounting to slavery, fuelled the efforts to resist this invasion. With the help of their French allies, the Government army repulsed this invading Rwandan Patriotic Front (RPF). This was followed by several brutal massacres of Tutsi and increasingly bloody guerrilla warfare over the following four years.

Several efforts to bring reconciliation between the two sides followed, culminating in formal peace talks in Arusha, Tanzania. In August 1993, President Habyarimana signed the Arusha Peace Accords agreeing to a form of power-sharing with the RPF. This was anathema to the hardliners, both on his side and amongst the RPF.

On 6th April 1994, President Habyarimana was killed when his plane was shot down as it was coming in to land at Kigali. This was immediately followed by a systematic slaughter of Tutsi and moderate Hutu who had opposed the government or had been attempting to find reconciliation. About 800,000 people were brutally slaughtered in 100 days, and 2 million refugees fled the country in what television reporters described as an exodus of biblical proportions. The refugee camps were places of horror, with terrible cholera epidemics where many more thousands died. Often the camps were under the control of the *interahamwe*, the militia who had killed so many in Rwanda. They made every effort to bring down the new Government of National Unity which was attempting to rebuild the stricken land.

As the RPF uncovered mass graves in Rwanda, there were many reprisal killings of Hutu, and one well-publicised massacre in the Kibeho camp, which had been set up by the French for Hutu refugees in the south of the country. In November 1994, the UN Security Commission set up the International Criminal Tribunal for Rwanda at Arusha, to try those who were guilty of organising the genocide.

For two years the *interahamwe* destabilised the country through serious violence near the Congo border in Gisenyi and Ruhengeri Prefectures. Thousands of Tutsi were murdered in raids across the border, and in their turn many Hutu, accused of sheltering the *interahamwe*, were killed by the RPF soldiers.

In 1996, the Rwandan army attacked these camps in Congo and the refugees swarmed back to their homes. To their surprise, most of the refugees were received back peacefully, although over the next few months, those who were accused of involvement in the genocide were imprisoned in appallingly over-crowded jails. It was easy to accuse an enemy, or someone whose job or home one coveted; as a result, many innocent people were imprisoned along with the truly guilty killers.

Over the next few years, the Government of National Unity did what it could to promote reconciliation in the country. They removed the ethnic classification from the national identity cards and said that there would be no further distinctions made on ethnic lines. The old quota system for schools and jobs based on ethnicity has been removed, and school places and jobs are now given officially on merit.

The judicial system had been decimated in 1994 with many judges either involved in the genocide or dead. It was difficult to start from scratch, and there was a long delay in bringing people to trial, with the prisons becoming ever fuller, resulting in an international outcry. Eventually some of the perpetrators of the genocide were put on trial, with the trials broadcast on national radio. Twenty-two of those found guilty were publicly executed in April 1998.

In an effort to deal with the over 125,000 prisoners, the Government decided to return to a form of the traditional justice system called *Gacaca*.[4] Local administrative areas selected people of good standing in every political area, and they were trained in judicial procedures. Large billboards appeared everywhere, proclaiming that if everyone admitted to what they had done and told what they had seen, the truth would save the country. The idea was that if people were tried in the *Gacaca* courts in their own locality, the truth would emerge.[5]

In 2003, many prisoners were unexpectedly released by presidential decree. Those released were in three categories:

1 Those who had no dossiers against them, and no case could be proved
2 Those who admitted their guilt and had served eight years in prison

3 The old and the sick or those who were under twelve years
   old when they were accused

After a time in rehabilitation camps they were sent home.
Throughout Rwanda the horror of 1994 was relived as some
of the perpetrators came back to the villages where they had
killed. The seeming normality of lives was again disrupted and
many were seriously traumatised, including some who
thought that they had forgiven.

Different elements of the history of Rwanda have caused
traumas which needed healing before forgiveness and reconciliation could take place. "To err is human, to forgive divine,"
proclaimed Alexander Pope.[6] Yet, with divine help, ordinary
human beings are able to forgive the most appalling harm.
God is beginning to restore the years that the locusts have
eaten.

Although few in the West have experienced such trauma,
we all need to learn the lessons of forgiveness. Some teach
that forgiveness is not an option for children who have been
abused, because the pain is too great and the sin so awful that
the perpetrator should have to suffer. The abused are told that
the process of forgiving is detrimental to their recovery and
emotional health, that it devalues their pain and sense of
worth. Some say that to expect forgiveness in a widow whose
husband has been murdered is inhuman. Forgiveness is hard
for the human mind to encompass. We want vengeance, even
though we know that violence tends to beget more violence,
as Rwanda shows; we want someone else to suffer in the way
that we have suffered. Christianity lived out in its shocking
fullness is something most of us cannot conceive. G K
Chesterton said of the Sermon on the Mount: "The Christian
ideal has not been tried and found wanting. It has been found
difficult and left untried."[7]

Rwanda has much to teach us in the West. Most Rwandan
Christians are trying to live a good life, truly believing the

Bible and the fact that Jesus died to bring forgiveness for their sins; but they do so without understanding the fullness of God's grace. The majority of those who have suffered huge loss are making every effort to put the pain behind them and resume their lives, living with the loss and trying to make sense of the future. Yet any reminder brings back the pain.

A growing body of people have experienced something more. They have seen the wonder of healing for their pain at the cross of Jesus and, having been healed, are finding the impossible becomes possible. They are forgiving those who caused them unbelievable harm. They are seeing their pain redeemed, and the locust years restored. Only God can give the capacity to forgive such appalling injuries, but he is doing it repeatedly throughout Rwanda. As men and women find their pain healed, the unforgivable can be forgiven through the power of the Holy Spirit. In place of the pain, he can release unspeakable joy, as murderer and victim meet together in the light of the cross. Only in such changed hearts is there hope for true reconciliation and the possibility that the cycle of hatred and vengeance will be broken.

Rwanda is a land of stark contrasts. The horrific events of 1994, with the systematic slaughter of over 800,000 people in 100 days and the flight of about 2 million refugees, has seldom been matched. The joy of those who know the healing that can be found at the cross, the forgiveness that releases them from anger and bitterness and enables them to bless those who harmed them, is almost unbelievable.

By no means has everyone in Rwanda been enabled to forgive in this way, but a growing number of people are exercising their God-given commission in the ministry of reconciliation. As Rwanda was once a byword for savagery and slaughter, may it once again be known as a land where God has shown his mercy and his glory, and where the locust years have been restored.

Notes

1. Not her real name
2. Not his real name
3. eg *Rwanda: The Land God Forgot?*, Guillebaud (London, Monarch, 2002). The Bradt travel guide to Rwanda has a readable section on the history, although Prunier's book, *The Rwanda Crisis: A History of Genocide* (London, C Hurst, 1995) is still the most complete.
4. Pronounced "Gachacha"
5. See chapter 7 for a fuller discussion of the *Gacaca* court system
6. *An Essay on Criticism*, 1711, l.525
7. G K Chesterton, *What's Wrong with the World*, 1910, ch. 5

CHAPTER TWO

The roots of prejudice

"See to it that no one fails to obtain the grace of
God; that no root of bitterness springs up and causes
trouble, and through it many become defiled."

(Hebrews 12:15, NRSV)

The origin of most of the violence in Rwanda
lies in ethnic prejudices that lead to injustice
and deep roots of bitterness, but such prejudices are common
throughout the world. Before sin introduced fear and prejudice against those different from us, God created men and
women in his own image. Just as he is Trinity, demonstrating
unity in diversity, he wanted humankind to demonstrate that
unity and diversity. He created not one sex but two, and
dozens of different races, each with its own language; yet
everyone was made in the image of God. The Bible clearly
teaches, and modern science appears to concur,[1] that geneti-
cally everyone in the world has descended from one woman,
Eve. Yet a frequently asked question is, "Why are we different?"

When the apostle Paul spoke to the Greek idol worshippers
of Athens, he described the creation of humankind in various
people groups with their own lands.[2] We adapted to our various
environments with different characteristics so that, for example, those with darker skin could live longer periods under
the sun than those with lighter skins; but we all came from
one blood. Our differences are only skin deep. God intended
that everyone should seek and find him, their Creator. Just as
our Triune God exists in relationships of love, he wants us to
demonstrate that same love in our relationships with one

another, though the prime relationship is a relationship of love towards God. The picture of God walking with Adam in the cool of the evening[3] speaks of the harmony God intended.

Sin destroyed that harmony. Initially, Adam and Eve were naked but unashamed.[4] They had no need to hide from each other or put on masks, but their first reaction after disobeying God was to sew leaves together in an effort to cover their nakedness.[5] Ever since, we have hidden our real selves from other people. They also hid from the God with whom they had enjoyed such a loving relationship.[6] Often when we have sinned, we no longer want to pray and enjoy fellowship with God. Our sins separate us from him.[7] They blamed each other, Satan and even God.[8] By their blame, they destroyed the fellowship they had previously enjoyed. Hiding from God, covering up our true selves and blaming one another have always been the consequences of sin.

The tree of the knowledge of good and evil led to the first sin with all its consequences. In giving the possibility of disobedience, God gave Adam and Eve the ability to choose. He wanted them to love him freely and obey him of their own free will. In the diversity he had created, conflict was inevitable, even before the Fall, as John Paul Lederach points out:

Adam and Eve were naming the animals and plants, feeding themselves, filling the earth, and being fruitful and multiplying. Can you imagine that they went about their tasks without disagreement and argument? Both were created in the image of God. Each was an individual, and each had freedom. Can you really imagine that they never argued or disagreed? How utterly boring, if that were the case! The Genesis story sets the stage for conflict as a natural part of our relationships because of who we are, as God created us. Conflict in itself is not sin. But sin may enter into the situation, depending on how we approach conflict, how we deal with it, and especially how we treat each other.[9]

The following chapters of Genesis show how sin destroyed relationships and the possibility of constructive conflict: the first recorded murder (4:1–10); the ground is cursed and harmony with the environment destroyed (4:11–13); polygamy begins and harmony in the home is destroyed (4:19); vengeance is seen as the best way of dealing with offence (4:23–24). By chapter 6 the world is so evil that God regrets having made it. Even after he starts afresh with righteous Noah and his family (9:1), his descendants in their pride soon build the tower of Babel. God scatters them, giving different languages so that they can no longer understand each other (11:1–9). No longer is there a harmonious whole, but the different groups murder and oppress each other. The different language groups develop different mindsets and begin fearing or despising each other. Xenophobia, fear of foreigners, led Pharaoh to subjugate the Hebrews in his land.[10]

God chose one group, the Hebrews, intending them to show the world how people should live in harmony, but they failed. Abraham's original call was in order that God could bless all the families of the world through him.[11] However, the Jewish people lost sight of that original purpose and regarded other nations as inferior, seeing themselves as God's chosen people. His Messiah was born of them, fulfilling Abraham's call and demonstrating God's love to all peoples.

Jesus died to enable new relationships; Calvary changed everything. Peter, a Jew, was amazed to find that even the Gentiles had received God's mercy. He needed a special vision from God to overcome his prejudices towards the Roman, Cornelius.[12] When he returned to Jerusalem he was criticised by his fellow Jewish believers for entering a Gentile's home, and in defence, he asked how, if God had accepted them, he could refuse them. "The Holy Spirit came on them as he had come on us at the beginning," he said. "So if God gave them the same gift as he gave us, who believed in the Lord Jesus Christ, who was I to think that I could oppose God?"[13] The

Jewish believers were amazed and praised God, saying, "So then, God has even granted the Gentiles repentance unto life!"[14]

However, not all the Jewish believers accepted this verdict. Acts 15 shows that some told the Gentile believers in Antioch that they had to keep the whole law of Moses and be circumcised to be accepted by God. This teaching affected even Peter. He had been eating quite happily with Gentiles before these believers came from Jerusalem, but for fear of offending them, he separated himself from the Gentiles and led others to do the same.[15] Paul challenged him about his hypocrisy. To him it was terrible to break table fellowship in this way. Later at the Council of Jerusalem,[16] Peter supported Paul in his defence of the Gentiles, stating that it is only by the grace of God that Jew and Gentile alike are saved.

Sadly, the history of the world is one of separating from, and despising, those who look or act differently from us. We each need to examine our prejudices, often excused as jokes against another ethnic group, for example, the Irish, Polish or Jews, and to see them as myths propagated by Satan, the father of lies, who robs us of the truth.

Dr Rhiannon Lloyd,[17] who has done much to bring healing and reconciliation to Rwanda, points out that the word "prejudice" literally means prejudgement. When we decide what someone else is like before we know that person, we are prejudging them. Jesus said, "Judge not, that you be not judged. For with what judgment you judge, you will be judged."[18]

Often we condemn in others our own unconscious sins. If we spend time thinking about a fault in another, we eventually become that which we judge; we reap what we sow.[19] This is why we are told to consider Jesus, in order that we become like him.[20] A critical spirit is harsh in its prejudices and blind to its own faults, and therein lies a big danger. Paul gives a very clear warning to this effect: "You, therefore, have no excuse, you who pass judgment on someone else; for at whatever point you judge the other, you are condemning yourself, because you who pass judgment do the same things. Now we know that God's judgment against those who do such things is based on truth."[21] If we want forgiveness from God, we must be prepared to look at others as he does without prejudice, accepting that we have faults as bad as theirs.

When we judge others, we are submitting to the law of God which says that we, too, will be judged. According to John Arnott, "If you demand justice and repayment for wrongs done to you then you will be dealt with according to your own prescription. The way you treat others is the way you will be treated."[22] He says that if we want grace and mercy from God, we must give grace and mercy to others, because when we judge them and speak critically of them, then we are placing ourselves in Satan's realm. He is called the accuser of the brethren,[23] and when we do his work we make ourselves vulnerable to his attacks through others. He cannot touch us when we are in God's realm of grace, mercy and forgiveness.

Arnott also points out that the broken bread at the communion table not only represents the broken body of our Lord Jesus Christ, but also his broken body, the church. The apostle Paul tells us that "anyone who eats and drinks without recognising the body of the Lord eats and drinks judgment on himself".[24] Commenting on this verse, Arnott says "We are his Bride, and his Body is precious to him. It grieves him deeply when we slander the Body of Christ by speaking against one another."[25] To do so means that we put ourselves back into the realm where Satan can judge us, rather than remaining beyond his touch under God's gracious protection.

> Judging is the opposite of graciousness [...] Judging and not forgiving are so closely connected that one could almost say that we judge partly because we haven't forgiven. For when we have totally forgiven it is surprising how quickly the temptation to judge is removed.[26]

Many attitudes are formed in childhood by parents and other significant adults. We are likely to disparage people we hear disparaged. If we hear them honoured, we will probably be at ease with them. What we hear about people influences us, as does how we ourselves were treated as children. A child from a secure and loving home will probably grow up secure and trusting. A child who has been abused and rejected will grow up suspicious and defensive. These attitudes will affect every contact he or she has with others, especially those who look different.

> If a child lives with criticism, he learns to condemn.
> If a child lives with hostility, he learns to fight.
> If a child lives with ridicule, he learns to be shy.
> If a child lives with shame, he learns to feel guilty.
> If a child lives with tolerance, he learns to be patient.
> If a child lives with encouragement, he learns confidence.
> If a child lives with praise, he learns to appreciate.
> If a child lives with fairness, he learns justice.
> If a child lives with security, he learns to have faith.
> If a child lives with approval, he learns to like himself.
> If a child lives with acceptance and friendship, he learns to find love in the world.[27]

Many children in Rwanda are growing up with the terrible scars of what they witnessed in 1994 and need healing of those memories. Prejudice about different groups is passed on from generation to generation. Jacqueline was born in Uganda of Tutsi parents who had fled Rwanda in the 1960s. Her home was filled with hatred for Hutu. From her earliest days, she was taught to hate, particularly by her old grandfather who died when he was 125 years old! He told her stories of Rwanda. "Hutu are not people," she was taught. "They don't look like us. They are incapable of love. They are totally bad." She loved her family cows, and her father added to her hatred of Hutu by telling her, from his experiences in 1959, "They hate cows. They enjoy slashing their legs and cutting them open. The only thing they like about cows is their meat."

She was fortunate in that they had enough money to send her to school, where for the first time she met Hutu. In her hatred, she refused to sit with them or eat with them. At home, she would tell her mother that she had been the only person in the minibus because the others were Hutu and therefore non-persons.

She was only twelve in 1990 when the RPF first invaded Rwanda. "Why am I still a child? If only I could join them. Nothing would give me more pleasure than to kill even one Hutu," she would think. She said something like this to her mother who was horrified by her hatred, and tried to beat it out of her. Her father was furious with her mother for that beating.

Soon after the genocide, she became a Christian. She wanted to go to Rwanda, but was frightened of meeting the Hutu. "What do they look like?" she asked her father. He said, "Look in a mirror. They look like you." She was appalled and became angry, with God, with herself, and still with the Hutu. Eventually she moved to the north of Rwanda but, although she was speaking as an evangelist, she still had nothing to do with Hutu. In church, she would not sit with them. She would not speak to one. If she saw one coming towards her, she would go the other way to avoid talking to him or her.

Faith in Jesus Christ should do away with divisions between Christians, whether of race or of status or of sex. "There is neither Jew nor Greek, there is neither slave nor free, there is neither male or female; for you are all one in Christ Jesus."[28] Yet how hard it is to change ingrained attitudes learnt in childhood.

Jacqueline found that the hatred in her heart was not automatically eradicated once she became a Christian. When she first went to an AEE seminar,[29] she saw Rhiannon, a European, and Anastase, a tall, good-looking Tutsi from Uganda. They were acceptable to her; but, to her horror, she saw that Anastase was with Joseph, a Hutu.

"Why is that Tutsi with that Hutu?" she wondered. "He must have been paid to come with him." She stood near the door because she was frightened that he would throw a grenade, and start to kill them. She listened in amazement, as Anastase explained that God made all people, that they were equal, and that we were intended to live together in harmony. She started to wonder whether it could possibly be true that even the Hutu could know God. Yet if they did, how could they kill in the way they had, and force her family to flee?

Then Joseph began to speak. "I am a Hutu from Gisenyi," he said. "I saw Hutu killing Tutsi. I know that my people took a pregnant woman and cut out her child. I know that my people threw old women into the longdrop latrines, so that they would drown in filth. I know that we did unspeakable things." Weeping, he added, "I am standing here on behalf of my people, to ask your forgiveness."

Jacqueline found it hard to believe that a Hutu was actually admitting the sins of his people, and weeping for them. As she listened, the hard place in her own heart began to melt. She felt the Lord saying to her, "All those times you said you wanted to kill a Hutu, are you not the same as him? Is there a difference? Are you not all murderers?"

She started to weep as well, and ran to her room where she found a new skirt she had hardly worn. She ran back to the meeting and up to Joseph. She flung the skirt at his feet and said, "I want you to know that here is a Tutsi woman who is giving you her forgiveness, and asking you for yours for the way she looked at Hutu. I want you to put this skirt in your bathroom, and when you and your wife and children come out of the shower, I want you to wipe your feet on it, and remember this Tutsi women who often killed Hutu in her thoughts. Please forgive me."

Joseph flung his arms round her and hugged her, the first

time she had been hugged by a Hutu, and he said, "Truly I forgive you. My children are small. Will you come to my home and become my oldest daughter?" She went to his home, and was welcomed by his family. She was able to put aside fears of poison and eat with them. She even visited his home in Gisenyi, at a time when it was still dangerous for a Tutsi to travel in that area. She was welcomed by Joseph's old mother and their neighbours. When night fell, she was nervous because marauding bands of Hutu were still coming over from Congo. "Can I trust this old woman to protect me? Will one of the neighbours betray me?" she asked herself, but she slept soundly and safely.

"I learned that Joseph was not the only good Hutu," she said. "Hutu are people just like us, with both good and bad amongst them. I, a Tutsi, am bad because I wanted to be rid of all Hutu. The fact that I did nothing actively doesn't alter my bad thoughts."

Notes

1. Mitochondrial DNA, drawn from five geographical populations, "all stem from one woman who is postulated to have lived about 200,000 years ago, probably in Africa". Cann RL, Stoneking M, Wilson AC; *Nature*, 1992 Apr 2; 356 (6368): pp 389–90. See also BBC News Reports, Wed 2 April 2003, by Paul Rincon and Wed 6 Dec 2000 by Dr David Whitehouse. For a fuller treatment of the subject see *Science*, 1996 Nov 29; 274 (5292): pp 1552–4.
2. Acts 17:24–27
3. Genesis 3:8
4. Genesis 2:25
5. Genesis 3:7
6. Genesis 3:8
7. Isaiah 59:2
8. Genesis 3:12–13
9. Lederach, 1999, pp 116–17
10. Exodus 1:8–11
11. Genesis 12:1–3
12. Acts 10 –

13. Acts 11:15,17 (NIV)
14. Acts 11:18 (NIV)
15. Galatians 2:11–13
16. Acts 15. I am aware that many scholars would put the writing of Galatians later but on balance I believe that it was written earlier than this Council since I cannot believe that Paul would not have referred to their conclusions had it been written later.
17. Dr Rhiannon Lloyd, a medical doctor trained in psychiatry, has spent time working in countries where there was ethnic violence, helping people recover from their inner wounds. See chapter 5 for the story of the AEE healing and reconciliation seminars.
18. Matthew 7:1–2a
19. Galatians 6:7
20. eg Hebrews 12:2–3; 1 John 3:2
21. Romans 2:1–2 (NIV)
22. Arnott, 1997, 2003, p 21
23. Revelation 12:10
24. 1 Corinthians 11:29 (NIV)
25. Arnott, 1997, 2003, p 37
26. Kendall, 2001, p 92
27. Dorothy Nolte's words as quoted by Anne Ortland in *Children are Wet Cement* (Old Tappan NJ, Fleming H Revell Company, 1981), p 58
28. Galatians 3:28
29. See chapter 5 for a description of these seminars

CHAPTER THREE

False ideas about forgiveness

"If you forgive men their trespasses, your heavenly Father will also forgive you. But if you do not forgive men their trespasses, neither will your Father forgive your trespasses." *(Matthew 6:14–15)*

Jacqueline learned that her evil prejudices needed forgiveness, even though she had not actually killed anyone. Yet she had not suffered in the way so many others have done in Rwanda. Is it possible to forgive unspeakable injuries?

Every time we say the Lord's prayer, we ask for God's forgiveness *as we forgive others* – but what does this mean? False ideas about forgiveness abound, yet it is central to the Christian faith, as Antoine Rutayisire, the Team Leader of African Evangelistic Enterprise (AEE),[1] found out. He describes what happened to him as a child in the 1960s in his book, *Faith under Fire*:

When I was five years old my father was butchered in broad daylight, before our very eyes, and left for dead in front of our house. He later on recovered, but was taken once more, and we never saw him again. We don't know how, where and when, or by whom he was killed. He was taken by the chief of our commune (county) with many other Batutsi and some suspected Bahutu accused of supporting the "enemy" and we were told they had been shot.

We never saw his body, we were never able to bury it. This kept us in a state of suspense for many years, hoping that maybe he had escaped and would come back some day. The death of a dear one is very difficult to accept when you have not witnessed it, or at least have evidence like a grave to prove it. I grew up thinking maybe my father was somewhere and would come back. When they talked of his death my young heart and mind could not accept it. Today I can understand many people who feel the same way, because they do not have any evidence of the death of their dear ones.

When I finally came to accept my father's death I turned my anger on the people I had seen beating my father and looting our possessions. Every time I had a problem I always remembered the massacre scene, and blamed my problem on the people. "If they had not killed my father, I wouldn't be faced with such a problem", was my simplified way of thinking.

I grew even to hate their children and I remember I used to persecute one of them who was with me in secondary school. He was far younger and did not even know what his father had done to mine. He could not understand why I hated him and I never took pains to explain.

Then during the massacres of 1972–73 we had to undergo a series of humiliating escapes, spending sleepless nights in hiding, uncertain of the future. I survived the experience, but this added to my list of enemies to hate. The tree of ethnic hatred in my heart was growing branches.[2]

Many of Antoine's relations were killed at that time. Eventually, he was able to go to university and became a lecturer at the National University of Rwanda at Butare. After a year, in 1983, the Government decided that there were too many Tutsi lecturers, and he was abruptly sacked. It was one more branch growing on the tree of hatred in his heart. One day, out of boredom, he started to read the Bible. He was gripped by it, and eventually read it through three times. He realised that forgiveness was central in what he had read, and that if he wanted to take the Bible seriously, he would have to forgive.

> It was easy for me to repent of many sins, but giving away my anger and bitterness against all those people who had offended me and my family was most difficult.
>
> But I was constantly confronted with the message of forgiveness and love of our enemies as conditional to being a child of God and having your prayers answered. The fellowship with God was becoming so precious to me that I did not want to jeopardise it by refusing to hand over my anger to God.[3]

To receive the forgiveness offered, Antoine would have to forgive the Hutu who had harmed him and his family. If he forgave, it would be a betrayal of his family and his people. Backwards and forwards went his thoughts, until eventually he knew that, whatever the cost, he had to forgive, if he wanted to continue in a deep relationship with God.

> Then one day I decided to take the bull by the horns and deal with the matter once and for all. I sat in my room, reread all the passages about the matter and decided I was going to comply with the Lord's requirements. I took a day alone and sat to forgive and pray for the Lord's blessing on all the people I hated. I made a list of all their names with all the wrongs each had done to me or to my family. Then I started declaring forgiveness to each, one by one and calling the Lord's blessing on them, their children, their businesses and their relatives.
>
> It was a very painful exercise and I had to do it again and again. But the result was tremendous. I was released and healed from the inside and I no longer felt the gripping pang of bitterness whenever one of the old "enemies" was mentioned in my presence.[4]

Early in 2003, Antoine met the daughter of the man who had been responsible for killing his father, when she came to see him in his office. She said that she had heard him speak at a meeting, saying that he forgave those who killed his father. "I need to hear you telling me to my face that you forgive," she said. "I forgave him the day I became a Christian," he replied. She had been repeatedly rejected as soon as people discovered her father's name, so she found it hard to accept that one of the victims could actually forgive her father and accept her. Antoine is still praying that she will find full release.

Antoine saw that forgiveness is at the very heart of the Christian faith. Rhiannon writes, "There is much misunderstanding about forgiveness within the church as well as in the world. Often we call something 'forgiveness' when it is not. True Biblical forgiveness is something far more profound and noble than most of us realise."[5] The only model for forgiveness is what God did for us on the cross through Jesus Christ. It cost him everything and shows how seriously God takes both sin and forgiveness. Any forgiveness that attempts to bypass the cross is not biblical forgiveness.

1 Forgiveness is not saying that it does not matter

For someone to say, "It does not matter", after we have struggled to ask forgiveness for something that may have caused offence, is deeply hurtful. Sin does matter, and we should never take it lightly. God certainly did not. He does not look at sin and say, "Let's forget about it." Sin cost him his Son. People often ask, "If I say that I forgive, does this mean that I am saying that it does not matter that my family was killed? If this is what God is asking of me, I cannot." God is not asking this, nor should we do it.

Exodus 34:6–7 tells us that God forgives wickedness, rebellion and sin. Then it goes on to say "... yet he does not leave the guilty unpunished ... "These statements seem to be contradictory. But "not leaving the guilty unpunished" is a poor translation of the original Hebrew. The literal translation is "cleanly he will not call the unclean clean". God can never call wrong right, but what he has done instead is to provide an atoning sacrifice. All sin has to be dealt with and cleansed by punishment or atonement – but it will never be condoned or overlooked.[6]

God, in his perfect righteousness, cannot dismiss sin. However long ago it was committed, sin remains sin. "If it was wrong when it happened, it is still wrong today, it will be wrong in 10 years time, it will still be wrong in 10 thousand years time. There will never be a time when sin is no longer sin."[7] The only ways to deal with it are by punishment or atonement. Someone has to pay. Jesus Christ did that for us on the cross, by taking the punishment we deserve, thereby atoning for our sin. If our sin cost so much, we must never treat it lightly. Sin matters, always.

2 Forgiveness does not mean pretending that we have not been hurt

Sometimes, people think that denying the effects of sin is the same as forgiveness. Many in Rwanda now want to put the events of 1994 behind them and resume their lives. They say they have forgiven, yet they are only repressing the pain. Because Rwandans are trained from early childhood not to show emotion, often they can describe horrendous events, like hiding beneath the bodies of their relations, and yet say that it had no effect on them. They say they are all right, but they have repressed the pain as a means of survival. We cannot forgive unless we accept that harm has been done to us and a wrong committed.

"Jesus tells us to forgive from the heart (Matthew 18:35).

It is very difficult to forgive from the heart while we are hiding pain in our hearts."[8] As John Gakwandi of Solace Ministries[9] said, "It is counter-productive to speak of forgiveness to hearts burdened with pain. They cannot forgive, and to tell them they should, makes them angry."

Jim Graham said, "To be a Christian is not to enter into some kind of fantasy land where we can escape some of the harsher and more painful realities of life. Christianity is not cheap escapism. As Christians we are compelled to face realities about ourselves, God, others, and the world around, and still have a living hope. Some, however, can only deal with an offence by pretending that it never happened. Wishing that it had never happened does not alter the fact that it did happen, damage has been done, and wounds have been inflicted, either by us or upon us."[10] As we face our pain and transfer it to Jesus, we can once again experience hope in a world that had seemed hostile to us.

Juliette is a Tutsi who was born into a Christian family in the South of Rwanda. While she was still a small child, her father fled from almost certain death when a Hutu government came in during the years following 1959. He went to Uganda leaving her mother to manage on her own. She grew up feeling a great sorrow because she had no father like the other children. She would ask her mother why her father could not be with them. Her mother told her what had happened to her father, and something of the history of the country, but always finished by saying, "There are good and bad people in every group, Tutsi, Hutu or Twa.[11] We are all people, with good and bad in each."

When she was twelve, Juliette became a Christian and was determined to marry another Christian, whatever his ethnic origin. As it happened, she married a Tutsi with whom she was able to share her pain from her childhood. "He took away my sorrow of a childhood without a father," she said. "He became a father to me as well as my husband; but, in 1994, he was killed by Hutu. Now I had no father and no husband. I began saying to myself, 'What have we Tutsi done? My mother must have hidden something from me. We must be very bad for them to keep on persecuting us in this way.' "

She began to deny that she was a Tutsi, because being a Tutsi had involved her in so much pain. She was hidden by a Hutu friend, who protected her throughout the dangers of that difficult time. Longing to ask her mother the questions she had, as soon as it was safe to travel, she went to look for her – only to find that her mother, too, had been killed. She looked for someone to tell her the nation's history, but could find no one she trusted to tell her the truth as she had trusted her mother.

She was consumed with pain as well as questions, and began to hate the Hutu who had stolen her family from her, even though she had been helped by a Hutu. Yet her Christian leaders and pastors told her that, as a Christian, she must forgive. "I sang in a choir," she said. "I smiled, but inside I was crying. When they told me to forgive and forget, that added to my pain. How could I forget the husband I lost, the father I never knew, my brothers, sisters, mother all dead? I felt that I could not be a true Christian, because the pain would not go away."

Joining AEE gave her colleagues who helped remove her loneliness, but the pain remained, hidden beneath a cheerful exterior. One week, a seminar[12] was held specifically for AEE staff. When she saw Anastase, she thought, "He has come from Uganda. What does he know of the pain of the survivors in Rwanda?" The other leader, Joseph, was a Hutu from Gisenyi, the worst area of killers. She despised them both, and refused to listen to the teaching on the first day.

The breakthrough came when she heard that it was acceptable to feel pain. When she wrote her story down, she wept and wept as never before. As she nailed her paper to the cross, she heard Jesus saying, "It is finished! All your pain, all your tears, all the impossibility to forgive, I have taken them and it is finished!"

The people in the seminar prayed for her for a long time. By next morning she felt better, and was able to listen to the teaching. For the first time, she found it possible to forgive those who had killed her loved ones. "Joy had come to replace the pain," she said. Now she wants to share with others what Jesus has done for her and to tell Christians that it is acceptable to feel pain, and that, although it is not easy, it is possible to forgive, the Holy Spirit helping.

3 Forgiveness cannot be commanded

The Lord's prayer says, "Forgive us our trespasses as we forgive those who trespass against us"; and many other passages in the Bible imply that if we do not forgive others, God will not forgive us.[13]

> It is not advisable to reduce forgiveness, or any other spiritual practice, to a moral obligation. If we do, we inevitably rob forgiveness of its free and spontaneous character. Yet some Christian practitioners advocate this approach [...] They think that they must perform an act of forgiveness before God will forgive them. They forget that God's forgiveness is not conditioned by puny human acts of forgiveness. How sad their view of God seems to be: a calculating and mercenary being, driven by the law of give and take.[14]

God forgave us our sins on the cross, when Jesus paid the penalty for them. In Ephesians 4:32 are these words: "forgiving one another, even as God in Christ forgave you". It is not that forgiving others is a precondition for forgiveness, but rather an example of how to forgive. God has already forgiven us, but we cannot receive that forgiveness until we come to him in repentance. He wants that forgiveness to flow out in forgiveness to others.

The unforgiving servant in Matthew 18:23–35, knowing

the immense debt he had been forgiven, did not practise mercy on his fellow servant. He did not allow the forgiveness he had received to work a change in his attitude, so his master gave him the punishment he deserved. The sombre challenge to us is: "So also my heavenly Father will do to every one of you, if you do not forgive your brother from your heart."[15] If we do not forgive others as we have been forgiven, we have not understood the full reality of that forgiveness.

> Most of us have been told things like, "Well, I don't care what they did. If you are a Christian, you have to forgive!" Sometimes forced forgiveness is only partial; it buries the wound without real healing. You don't have to forgive. You can hold on to it if you like, but understand the dynamics.
>
> You are entitled to justice, but then you will also reap what you have sown. You, too, will receive what you deserve instead of mercy. When I understood that, I knew what Jesus meant when he said, in Matthew 5:7 "Blessed are the merciful, for they will be shown mercy."[16]

Juliette had been told she had to forgive as a Christian, yet until her pain had been addressed, she was unable to do so. As she saw that Jesus had died to give her joy and healing for her sorrow and wounded heart, so she was set free to forgive.

When he says the Lord's prayer, Monbourquette "... recite(s) it thinking of St Paul's words: 'you must forgive as the Lord forgave you' (Colossians 3:13). In the same vein, a friend told me of her preference for the following: 'Forgive us our trespasses so that we may forgive those who have trespassed against us.' "[17] This petition suggests that the Holy Spirit will enable us to follow his example in forgiving others, yet, it is hard to escape the many verses[18] that say that if we do not forgive, God will not forgive us. How can we forgive from a heart filled with pain, as Juliette's? Neither can we forgive if our hearts are full of hatred.

4 "Forgive and forget"

> When we try to forget the wrongs we have suffered, we lose
> our perspective on our personal history. In many cases, we are
> trying to create a less distressing and disappointing past.
> Because we are terrified that we cannot face the past without
> being overwhelmed by pain, we never taste the wonder of
> God's forgiveness – both of our sin and the sins of those who
> have harmed us.[19]

Rwandans often think that, if they allow themselves to remember the horrific events that caused their pain, they will lose their forgiveness. Rhiannon asked one lady what had happened to her in 1994. She replied, "Please don't ask me, because I have forgiven, and if I remember, I will no longer be able to forgive." While it was not in her mind, she felt she had forgiven.

On 7th April 2004, at a memorial service for members of his family who had been killed on the first day of the genocide, Wilberforce's[20] son, John, stood by his mother's grave. He cried out, "I have been told to forgive and forget. How can I forget what happened here to my mother, my brothers and my sister!" I replied, "God is not asking you to forget, indeed he has not forgotten what happened here, nor your anguish; but, for your sake you need to forgive and, as you forgive, you will find that you can remember in a different way and resolve to do all you can so that it will never happen again."

> Forgiving and forgetting are related, but forgiving precedes
> forgetting. To forgive, one must first remember the injury, the
> impact, the injustice done.
>   To forget ignores the needs of the offender and injures the
> offended by driving the sense of being wronged deep into
> one's own being where resentment does its slow destructive
> work. Forgetting is negative, passive; forgiving is positive and
> creative.[21]

Until we forgive someone who has caused us harm, we cannot bear to think positively about that person. Having forgiven, we can talk about the events without the sting. Many Rwandans have been enabled to forgive terrible harm committed against them or their families. When something brings back the memory, they say, "I remind myself that I have been forgiven through the blood of Jesus. That by an act of my will I have forgiven and I continue to stand on that forgiveness and to act it out." The memory is still there but without the pain.

Some people say that because God forgets our sin, we should forget what others have done to us. God has not forgotten that we are sinners. If we have transferred our sins on to the Lord Jesus, God sees them on him and not on us. This is not forgetting them, but remembering them in a different way. Unlike God, humans are incapable of forgetting. We might bury memories and refuse to think about them, but an unexpected sound, smell or sight can bring them back as fresh as if they happened yesterday. We, too, need to remember differently, with the pain and bitterness of the memories taken away.

Throughout Rwanda are Genocide Memorial sites with the expressed intention of reminding people of the horror, so that it can never happen again. Where true forgiveness has been granted, they may never forget, but the remembrance is redemptive.

5 Forgiveness is not excusing what the other has done

"I forgive him because it's not his fault. He was badly damaged as a child and is reacting out of his hurt." Statements such as these tend to confuse the issue. A wrong action is always wrong, and must not be excused. Understanding why someone did something may help us to forgive, but that is not the same as excusing their behaviour. "Excusing them means absolving them of all moral responsibility. There is no limit to the number of pretexts used for these excuses: heredity, education and prevailing culture are among them. At this rate, no one would be responsible for their actions since no one would be free enough. This is a warped interpretation of the saying 'To understand all is to forgive all.' "[22]

In Genesis 18, when Abraham pleads for Sodom, he does not excuse the behaviour of those in Sodom but appeals to the character of God. "Shall not the Judge of all the earth do right?"[23] When God wants to destroy the people of Israel, both at Mount Sinai when they had worshipped a golden calf in place of God (Exodus 32) and at Kadesh Barnea when they refused to trust God and enter the Promised Land (Numbers 14), Moses does not excuse the behaviour of the people. Rather, he is concerned for God's reputation, and appeals to his character and his mercy. God had mercy on Lot and his family and forgave the Israelites, although he punished them.

One can understand why the Hutu feared a return to Tutsi-dominated rule, and why they were influenced by the hate messages on the radio dehumanising and demonising the Tutsi; but that does not excuse their actions in killing. One can understand a Tutsi soldier hearing of massacres taking place elsewhere in the country going berserk and killing in reprisal; but he is morally responsible for his actions. Understanding may help us to reach the point of forgiveness, but it does not excuse the actions.

6 Forgiveness does not mean that we should not seek justice through the courts

Many Rwandans believe that forgiveness means that the wrongs forgiven will have no consequences. They feel that Romans 12:17–19 and 1 Corinthians 6:1–8 both teach that no Christian should go to law, yet Romans 13:1–5 clearly states that the judicial system is God's instrument for keeping peace in society. "It was God's idea for there to be a just judicial system in every nation for the protection of society. God says to us, 'Where you are concerned, don't take justice into your own hands by seeking revenge, but instead seek to bless them. Let the judiciary system of the nation take its own course.' "[24]

7 Forgiveness does not mean peace at any price

In Matthew 18:15–17, Jesus tells us that when a Christian has sinned against us, we must go to him or her and point out the fault, so that we can continue in fellowship. The other may be unaware of the offence caused. It is much easier to say, "I will forgive, and forget about it." However, if we see the person again, often the resentment recurs, and we have, in effect, "lost a brother".

Sometimes the sin is of a serious nature, and threatens either the unity or the purity of the church. If the Christian who has sinned refuses to accept his fault, the church must take action, and if necessary expel the offender, that the integrity of the body may be preserved. The reason for this expulsion is to bring about repentance and restoration of the offender (2 Corinthians 2:5–8). This means that our attitudes towards church discipline are very important. In Galatians 6:1–3, Paul talks of correcting others in a spirit of gentleness and love, recognising that we too are sinners, rather than having an attitude of self-righteous indignation. However difficult confrontation may be, for the sake of the church it must not be neglected. Paul did not hesitate to confront Peter with his hypocrisy when he saw how it threatened the unity of the infant church, when Peter, for fear of the Pharisees in the church, drew back from eating with Gentiles.[25] Nor did Peter hesitate to confront Ananias and Sapphira when their lies and self-interest threatened the purity of the infant church.[26]

8 Forgiveness does not mean leaving it to God

"Only God can forgive." No doubt you have heard this line spoken as if human beings had no place in the act of forgiveness. This makes a nice pretext for passing all of one's responsibilities on to God! But it would be wrong to do so, since in the realm of forgiveness, as in any other, God doesn't do for us what is up to us to do. Recently, someone was telling me how easy it was for them to forgive: 'If someone hurts me, I quickly ask God to forgive them. That way, I don't have to be disturbed by all sorts of feelings of pain, resentment or humiliation.' As admirable as this demonstration of faith may be, it raises questions about the mental health of the individual who is doing the forgiving. Instead of taking charge of life, as painful as this may be, the person hands it over to God.[27]

Asking God to forgive someone for a hurtful action is superfluous. We were forgiven by God when Jesus cried out on the cross, "Father, forgive them." The trouble is that, in order to receive that forgiveness, we need to accept that his death was for us, and be prepared to forgive others. If we refuse to forgive as God has forgiven, we cannot receive his forgiveness. God wants us to forgive as he has forgiven us, and to pray for the person we have forgiven, blessing him or her,[28] but that is not the same as asking him to forgive the person. That is for us to do, helped by his Holy Spirit.

When Stephen was dying, stoned by an angry mob, he cried out, "Lord, do not hold this sin against them."[29] He was standing in the gap on their behalf, willing to accept the consequences of their actions instead of them. He showed his forgiveness, and asked God to withhold his wrath against them, but he was not asking God to forgive them without doing so himself.

9 Forgiveness does not necessarily mean reconciliation

Aimable is the local team leader for the AEE Healing and Reconciliation Team at Nyamata. He is a charismatic Roman Catholic who has been conducting seminars throughout the country in Catholic churches. He is a Tutsi, whose family was displaced to Nyamata in 1959 when he was three years old. Most of his family was killed at Nyamata in one of the worst massacres of 1994. The bones of his mother and sisters are amongst those in the Memorial site there. He had managed to flee from the killing in the church, but came back as soon as possible, only to see the body of one sister outside. She had had her hands and feet tied and had obviously been raped repeatedly before she was slashed across her body and left to die. He subsequently hid from the killers in the swamp for three weeks. For some time after the genocide he was in total despair, filled with a rage against all Hutu, and crippled with the agony of loss. His anger was particularly focussed on one Hutu neighbour. "He was my friend," he said, "but he stole my shop and everything in it, leaving me with no means of support."

Aimable went to the first meeting of the Christian survivors in Nyamata in 1994, when Rhiannon Lloyd first arrived in Rwanda. There he heard of the depth of the love of God our Father. He realised that God wanted to be his Father and that he wanted him to forgive as the Lord Jesus had forgiven him, yet he could not. It was not until he went to a full seminar in 1996, that he was able to nail his pain and anger to the cross, and to forgive fully. For the first time he was able to sleep that night.

In particular, he forgave that one who had been the focus of his anger. He had fled to Congo, but when Aimable heard that he had returned, he went to find him, to tell him that he had forgiven him. "Do you expect me to respond?" was the reply. "No, I wanted to tell you, for my part, that you are forgiven." He did not receive that forgiveness, but Aimable felt released from him. "I know the healing I have received through forgiving," he said, "and I now want to help as many others as I can to learn to forgive." Unusually, he knows those who killed his family, but, as they are refugees, he has not been able to tell them that he has forgiven them.

Ideally reconciliation follows forgiveness, but it is not always possible. The majority of those in Rwanda never knew who murdered their loved ones. Frequently, a victim has been able to forgive without knowing the identity of the killer. Often, it is impossible to restore a relationship where none previously existed. Indeed, sometimes reconciliation is inadvisable, for example in the case of sexual abuse, even though the victim has forgiven. Between Christians, true forgiveness must restore fellowship wherever possible, but for reconciliation to take place there must be movement on both sides, repentance on the one hand and forgiveness on the other.[30]

Jesus said, "Take heed to yourselves. If your brother sins against you, rebuke him; and if he repents, forgive him. And if he sins against you seven times in a day, and seven times in a day, returns to you saying, 'I repent', you shall forgive him."[31] Matthew adds, "If he hears you, you have gained your brother."[32] Reconciliation has taken place. This can only happen between brothers, or Christians, who share the same premises for forgiveness based on the cross of Jesus. Without that common starting point, it is difficult, if not impossible, to reach reconciliation.

Martin[33] was released by presidential decree in January 2003. In prison he had become a Christian, accepted his guilt and confessed it before a court. He had killed some children during the genocide, and said, "I am nervous about what lies ahead as I return home. I must meet the family I betrayed, who are neighbours and unbelievers. I have asked for their forgiveness but they have refused it." He is trusting God for the future but many uncertainties remain. How can he continue to live near those whose family he killed?

Although many of the stories in this book are of forgiveness and reconciliation, not all have forgiven. It requires much faith to continue in the consciousness of appalling guilt, as Martin did, and still proclaim the love and forgiveness of God.

10 "No forgiveness without restitution"

In South Africa many are saying that it is not possible to forgive unless the offender has confessed, and offered restitution. The experience of many in Rwanda would refute this. No restitution is possible for those who have lost their families. Even in South Africa, many are saying that to put a price on their suffering is impossible, but a person who truly repents will be willing to make any restitution possible. Only God can judge who is truly repentant, but we can often see the fruit.[34]

A man who had killed several members of a woman's family became a believer in prison through the preaching of Method, the International Director of Youth with a Mission in Rwanda. On a later visit, he said that he knew God had forgiven him, but he had no peace until he knew that his victim knew that he was repentant. He asked Method to seek her out and ask her for forgiveness on his behalf. When Method found her, she was overjoyed. "I too have become a Christian," she said, "and I have been praying for the killer ever since." She asked Method to accompany her to the prison, where there was true reconciliation, with both of them in tears. Afterwards, she visited him twice a week taking him the food he needed, as proof of her forgiveness. He could make no restitution at that stage, although he was willing; amazingly she was the one who ended up blessing him! Forgiveness releases the victim from the bonds of bitterness towards the offender. In some way in the heavenly places, forgiveness also releases the offender, and opens his or her heart to the gospel of Christ.

Notes

1. One of many Christian organisations fully involved in working for healing and reconciliation in Rwanda
2. Rutayisire, 1995, p 105–6
3. Ibid, p 107
4. Ibid, pp 107–8
5. Lloyd with Bresser, 2001, p 73
6. Ibid
7. Ibid
8. Ibid
9. One of the many Christian organisations involved in the work of healing and reconciliation in Rwanda
10. Graham, 1991, p 10
11. The Twa are the third ethnic group in Rwanda, usually despised by both Hutu and Tutsi
12. See chapter 5 for a description of this seminar
13. See Matthew 6:12–15; Mark 11:25; Luke 6:37
14. Monbourquette, 2000, pp 35–6
15. Matthew 18:35 (RSV)
16. Arnott, 1997, 2003, p 55
17. Monbourquette, 2000, p 36
18. Matthew 6:14–15; 18:21–35; Mark 11:25
19. Dan Allender, in his chapter on the Myths of Forgiveness in the book *God and the Victim*, Lampman, Lisa Barnes (ed) et al, 1999
20. His story is told in chapter 1
21. Frank Stagg, quoted by Augsburger, 1988, p 45, from *Polarities of Man's Existence in Biblical Perspective* (Philadelphia, Westminster, 1973) p 161
22. Monbourquette, 2000, p 39
23. Genesis 18:25
24. Lloyd with Bresser, 2001, p 77. See chapter 7 for a fuller treatment of this subject
25. Galatians 2:11–14
26. Acts 5:1–11
27. Monbourquette, 2000, p 41
28. Luke 6:27–28
29. Acts 7:60 (NRSV). See chapter 6 for a discussion of the term "standing in the gap"
30. This subject will be dealt with more fully in chapter 11
31. Luke 17:3–4

32. Matthew 18:15
33. Not his real name
34. Luke 3:8

CHAPTER FOUR

What is true forgiveness?

"Put on then, as God's chosen ones, holy and beloved, compassion, kindness, lowliness, meekness, and patience, forbearing one another and, if one has a complaint against another, forgiving each other; as the Lord has forgiven you, so you also must forgive."

(Colossians 3:12–13, RSV)

We can only truly forgive, if we understand what Christ has done for us and have received that forgiveness, but true forgiveness is costly. It cost God his Son. It can only be achieved by his grace.

God's grace showed Agnes that she needed forgiveness. In 1959, when in her third year of school, her parents moved to Kiramuruzi,[1] fleeing massacres further south. She was told that, as a Tutsi, she could not continue in school. She married at the age of 17, and had a total of seven children. In 1994 when the killing began, the local government officer for their area was rabidly anti-Tutsi, and Kiramuruzi became the scene of terrible massacres. In a few days, hundreds of Tutsi were killed, together with many Hutu who refused to take part in the killing.

As soon as she heard the news of the President's death, Agnes and her family fled to a Hutu neighbour's house. She hid all nine of them, but once the *interahamwe* had killed everyone they could find, they began searching the houses. Their protector asked them to leave or she, too, would be killed, so they fled to the church for safety. On the way, her husband and one of her sons were killed.

Unlike what happened elsewhere in the country, the roving gangs of *interahamwe* terrified but did not harm them in the church, perhaps because the RPF came so soon. Hearing that they were close, Agnes and others fled to a nearby hill where they were found by the RPF, and taken back to Kiramuruzi. Her house had been destroyed; so, as most of the Hutu had fled, she moved into one of their houses.

A group of Christian Unity was formed, consisting of Christians of both ethnic groups who wanted to demonstrate a new way of life. They used to visit Agnes and pray for her until she felt she could go back to church. At first, she could not even look at a Hutu without fear, but gradually that fear subsided. In the church, she learned about forgiveness. Her husband's killer was arrested and although Agnes refused to accuse him, others did and he is still in prison, refusing to accept his guilt.

Agnes was helped to forgive by teaching from MOUCECORE,[2] who encouraged and prayed for her; by the comfort and practical help of Christian friends; by God's word; by the Christian Unity Group which she joined; by the government's emphasis on reconciliation. She also recognised her own need for forgiveness, having stolen a cow from a Hutu neighbour. She asked for her forgiveness and they are now close friends. "Because I have received God's grace," she said, "I want to extend that grace to others so that true reconciliation between God and man, and between Hutu and Tutsi, can be found. I was only able to forgive when I had been comforted by God."

God's grace reminded Stephanie that she had received mercy at the hands of her enemy. A Hutu, brought up in Kiramuruzi, she became a follower of Christ in 1973 at a local school meeting. When the genocide began in 1994, she was married with two children and was expecting her third. On the morning of 7th April, she went to dig in her fields as usual. As soon as she heard the news, she knew war was imminent. The Hutu were called to a big meeting in the town where weapons were handed out. She left and went home, refusing to leave. She saw many Tutsi fleeing, and hid some in her fields until it was no longer safe to do so.

Later, hearing that the RPF were nearby, she and her husband, with their parents and children, fled. The RPF caught them on 15th May, and killed both her husband and father. The soldiers threatened to kill her, too. She was terrified to show them that she was pregnant, because she had heard that they enjoyed ripping babies out of pregnant women. They tried to force her to drink some sorghum beer[3] but she refused, saying she was a Christian. She was told to lie down and one soldier ground his gun into her head by her ear. When he removed the gun, he asked if she was a true Christian. She said, "Yes". He ordered her to go and milk the cow. Having given the milk to the soldiers, they told her to look after her children and left.

They had stolen all her possessions, but she knew that God was looking after her, and would continue to do so. She gave birth a few days later, in a refugee group at Kiramuruzi. Her father-in-law refused to have anything further to do with her, because her husband, his son, was dead.

Stephanie took on responsibility for ten orphans, as well as her own children. She was helped, both spiritually and practically, by the Christian Unity group in her church, as well as by the teaching from MOUCECORE. She realised that she had received mercy, both from the RPF soldiers and God; this helped her forgive.

The true basis of forgiveness was well summed up by two clergymen, Steven and Tito, from Burundi, where they have the same ethnic divisions as in Rwanda. "If we have been saved by the cross of Jesus Christ, how can we look at other people, even killers, except through his eyes?" This was Paul's comment in 2 Corinthians 5:16 (RSV) when he said, "From now on, therefore, we regard no one from a human point of view." Paul goes on to say that, "in Christ God was reconciling the world to himself, not counting their trespasses against them, and entrusting to us the message of reconciliation."[4]

Steven was a Tutsi whose family were killed in 1993, following the killing of the first Hutu president. Eighteen members of his immediate family were slaughtered, and he and his polio-crippled wife fled to the home of Tito, a Hutu who sheltered nearly a hundred Tutsi during that terrifying time. In the reprisals that took place after the army regained control, Tito's eldest son was killed by Tutsi. Once relative peace was restored, it was found that Steven's house had been destroyed, so he and his wife continued to live with Tito for the following four years. Many people, both Hutu and Tutsi, objected. "How can you live with those who killed your family?" they would ask. Both replied in almost identical words. "It is because we are saved." Steven said, "I no longer see Hutu or Tutsi, but only the family of God." Tito added, "I am not bitter because Jesus died for me. My son was killed in war, not by Tutsi. As people of God, we want to show God's love to everyone."

Forgiveness cost God his Son. In some way we cannot explain, he was actually in Christ on the cross, and yet at the same time separate, when Christ, the sinless one, became sin for us. The cross is often sanitised, a gold ornament in a church or hanging round our necks, but the original cross was brutal beyond description, as Mel Gibson's film, *The Passion of the Christ*, makes graphically clear. It was intended to dehumanise the victims. Derek Prince in his book, *Atonement*, marvels at the restraint of the Gospel accounts that simply state that Jesus was crucified, without going into the detail of that film. For example, Luke points out that the women who followed him stood at a distance,[5] because Jesus would have been totally naked. Passers-by were encouraged to taunt and do whatever unspeakable things took their fancy to any crucified man, and Jesus was no exception.

Quintillian (c AD 35 – c AD 100) describes crucifixion in a letter: "Whenever we crucify the guilty, the most crowded roads are chosen, where most people can see and be moved by this fear. For penalties relate not so much to retribution as to their exemplary effect."[6] Seneca (c 4 BC – c AD 65), the Roman historian, felt that it would be better for someone to commit suicide rather than go through the agony of crucifixion. "Can anyone be found who would prefer wasting away in pain dying limb by limb, or letting out his life drop by drop, rather than expiring once for all? Can any man be found willing to be fastened to the accursed tree, long sickly, already deformed, swelling with ugly wounds on shoulders and chest, and drawing the breath of life amid long drawn-out agony?"[7] Yes, one man was found willing to die in such a way – and he did it for us.

More than all that humiliation and pain, the true horror our Lord Jesus endured was in becoming sin for us. He cried out, "My God, my God, why have you forsaken me?"[8] For the first time in his sinless existence, communication with his Father was broken. All sin breaks communication with God,[9] and when Jesus became sin for us, he went through what St John of the Cross calls "the dark night of the soul", when he could no longer sense his Father's presence. He did it for us.

If forgiveness was so costly for God, it cannot be easy for us either. It involves acknowledging our pain, and taking it to the cross, as well as facing our own sin and placing that on Jesus, as Agnes did. As a result God does not count our sin against us. All penalties against us are cancelled, because Jesus Christ accepted those penalties instead of us – one of the wonderful exchanges that took place at the cross.[10]

God has entrusted to us the message of reconciliation, and this is the only hope for Rwanda. Yet, when we think of some of the atrocities committed, is it not sadistic of God to expect the victims to forgive? Are some things not too awful? We cannot forgive until we have received God's forgiveness with its releasing power and truly understood what that means. Unforgiveness, however, leads to bitterness in our hearts, which can in turn lead to physical sickness. It binds us to those who have harmed us, and enables Satan to have power over our lives.[11] Only by forgiving are we released.

Nora's husband, Wilberforce,[12] said, "They are not repentant. If I forgive, it only sets them free to do it again." Many ask that question. "What if the perpetrator does not repent? Perhaps he even boasts of what he did; does God *still* expect me to forgive?" On the cross, the Lord Jesus forgave while the soldiers were driving the nails into his hands and mockingly casting lots for his clothing.[13] How could he forgive those who were enjoying what they were doing? Surely a real man would be cursing them, as did one thief. Instead of retaliating, "he trusted to him who judges justly."[14]

It is extremely hard to forgive those who show no evidence of repentance, unless we believe that they will face judgement before a just God. Questions of justice and punishment can safely be left to God, the righteous judge. We cannot possibly decide whether someone has truly repented. What punishment is adequate for the torture and death of those whom we love? Such questions can only lead to a desire for vengeance and further bitterness. The only safe place to put these questions is in the hands of God who is truly just and overflowing in mercy.

The shocking thing about the way that Jesus forgave is that, not only did he entrust all thoughts of revenge to God who says, "Vengeance is mine, I will repay,"[15] but he also interceded for those who were causing his pain, as well as for us whose sin was placed upon him. "He bore the sin of many, and made intercession for the transgressors."[16]

Many Rwandans died like Jesus, praying for their murderers. Some asked for time to pray a blessing on them. This frightened some of the killers, who left them alone. Others became even more enraged and killed brutally. Occasionally, killers became believers by seeing their victims die with hope, often singing hymns or praying for their killers. "They died with the Holy Spirit on them," they say.

Some Roman Catholic nuns were running an orphanage when the killers came and asked for the Tutsi children to be handed over. The nuns replied, "We have neither Tutsi nor Hutu here but only children of God." Enraged, the killers marched them all out to a mass grave, where the nuns started the children singing a hymn of praise. The nuns were killed first, but the children went on singing to the last one.

True forgiveness is not easy, but it is extremely powerful.

1 Forgiveness means refusing to take revenge

"This is the essence of total forgiveness. It is when we give up the natural desire to see them 'get what's coming to them'. By nature we cannot bear the thought that they have got away with what they have done; it seems so unfair,"[17] says R T Kendall, speaking of the refusal to take private vengeance in destroying the reputation of the one who has harmed us. The State should nevertheless decide the punishment of those who have offended against state laws.

Three times in the Bible God says "Vengeance is mine. I will repay."[18] If we seek to exact our own vengeance, we are usurping God's role, which he hates. It shows that we do not trust him to do right. Relinquishing our right to take revenge means that we choose not to spread the news of what our enemy has done. This is not to say that we refuse to testify in court, or even to tell others how God has enabled us to forgive, but we refuse to take someone's reputation away. We leave all questions of revenge in God's hands.

When we are hurting, most of us cannot cope with Jesus' command to love our enemies. "Do good to those who hate you, bless those who curse you, pray for those who abuse you."[19] God might take us at our word, and bless those who have harmed us so badly! Once our pain has been healed, which may take time, we are in a position to consider forgiveness. If we have truly forgiven, the Holy Spirit will enable us to pray for, and even to bless, our enemies. Many of these stories have shown Rwandans who have been enabled, not only to pray a blessing on their abusers, but in some cases actually to provide the blessing themselves. However, if we can bring ourselves to pray for our enemies and determine to forgive them, even in the midst of our pain, this can hasten the process of healing. There is a circle of healing: healing pain enables forgiveness; determination to forgive enables healing.

2 Forgiveness involves an act of the will; it is not merely a feeling

Forgiveness is not a feeling, but a deliberate choice of the will. Feelings may come later, but when we choose to say aloud, "Lord, I forgive the one who has done such harm", that person's power to hurt leaves.

Even so, forgiveness takes more than willpower. Children are often told to "say sorry and make up". "At that age, we never thought to doubt the value of such an artificial form of forgiving. The words came out of our mouths, but our hearts were not in them. Such forgiveness likely did more to soothe the teacher's nerves than to educate the child."[20] The will is probably not involved in such facile acts of forgiveness.

"Will is, of course a big part of the picture, but alone it cannot do the job of forgiveness. Forgiveness mobilizes all of our faculties: sensitivity, the heart, intelligence, judgment, imagination, and so on."[21] As Juliette[22] found when she was told to "say sorry and make up", she exercised her will and said the words, but her pain festered. However, forgiveness starts with the will, with the decision to forgive.

Part of that decision is to keep no record of the wrong done against us. "Love 'keeps no record of wrongs' (1 Cor 13:5).

Why do we keep records? To use them. To prove what happened. To wave it before someone who doubts what happened [...] Love is a choice. Total forgiveness is a choice. It is not a feeling – at first – but an act of the will. It is the choice to tear up the record of wrong."[23] We need to make the choice not to keep a physical record of the harm done, unless, of course, for the sake of society we need to take a case to court.

It is equally important not to keep a mental tally of the wrongs done. It is often the accumulation of unforgiven hurts which can break a marriage or any other relationship.

Jonathan Aitken found it hard to forgive the reporters who persistently told scurrilous lies about him. He met a monk who was a chaplain in Belmarsh prison who told him, "Pray to receive the gift of forgiveness, and when you receive it, give the gift back towards those towards whom you feel unforgiving."[24] As we have received the gift of God's forgiveness, we need to ask his help to turn it back to those who have harmed us, and to make us willing to see them blessed as we have been blessed ourselves.[25]

3 Forgiveness means facing reality

None of those whose stories are told here doubt the atrocities committed against them, but it is possible to deny our hurts, or to excuse what the other has done, saying, "She didn't really mean it!" True forgiveness involves acceptance of the harm, as well as relinquishing the right to revenge.

"Total forgiveness is painful. It hurts when we kiss revenge goodbye. It hurts to think of that person getting away with what they did and nobody knowing. But when I know fully what they did and accept in my heart that they will be blessed without any consequences for their wrong, I have crossed over into the supernatural. This means I have begun to be a little like Jesus."[26]

4 Forgiveness involves accepting and even forgiving ourselves

Often, beside the hurt of betrayal is a self-loathing for allowing ourselves to be taken in, or manipulated. Perhaps we have even contributed to the offence. In facing that squarely, we may need to forgive ourselves and, if necessary, repent.

In many situations, such guilt is false. This needs to be faced and our true part in the tragedy accepted. Many Tutsi felt that there was something wrong with them to cause the suffering they had experienced. A rape victim often feels shame and considers that she must somehow have asked for it. The same happens to victims of child abuse. Before we can truly forgive the perpetrator, we must accept ourselves, facing the true reality of the sin committed against us.

5 Forgiveness means recognising God's love and justice

Most of our bitterness is, at root, a bitterness aimed at God. "Why? Because he allowed bad things to happen. Since he is all-powerful and all-knowing, he could have prevented these things from happening. He has allowed us to suffer when we didn't do anything that we know of to warrant such ill-treatment. Therefore what we are ultimately thinking is that God is to blame for our hurt."[27]

Job's suffering was apparently because of a wager in heaven. He was unable to understand why he was suffering. Initially, he rebukes his wife who tells him to "curse God and die". He says, "Shall we indeed accept good from God, and shall we not accept adversity?"[28] As time goes on, his need for self-justification grows; yet when God finally reveals his power and majesty, even though he never answers his questions about suffering, Job's reaction is to say, "I have uttered what I did not understand ... therefore I abhor myself, and repent in dust and ashes."[29] We may never know why God allowed us to go through our particular suffering but we can affirm his love and his justice. Part of true forgiveness is repenting of any residual bitterness we may hold against God.

Yet our questions are real, and need to be faced. "How can a God who loves me have allowed me to experience so much suffering?" or, "How can a just God allow so much injustice in the world?" or even, "How can an all-powerful, all-loving God have allowed the genocide, or the 2004 tsunami in South Asia?" Job challenged God and was found righteous; his "comforters" tried to defend God and were shown to be at fault. The disciples, meeting the risen Lord Jesus on the mountain, "worshipped Him; but some doubted".[30] It is unbelief, not doubt, that is the opposite of faith. But doubts need to be faced. If we bury them in our hearts, they can fester and turn into unbelief.

At the start of their seminars the AEE team look at some of these questions:[31]

1 "How can a God who loves me have allowed me to experience so much suffering?"
People who have experienced deep pain often feel that a God who expects them to forgive the one who caused such pain must be sadistic. They have many questions: "We did nothing to deserve atrocities." "Often it was simply because we were born Tutsi." "Can God possibly love us?" C S Lewis faced similar questions about God's love after his wife died. "Not that I am (I think) in much danger of ceasing to believe in God. The real danger is of coming to believe such dreadful things about him. The conclusion I dread is not 'So there's no God after all' but 'So this is what God's really like. Deceive yourself no longer.' " His next question was, "Is it rational to believe in a bad God? Anyway, in a God as bad as that? The cosmic Sadist, the spiteful imbecile?"[32]

We live in a fallen world, in which everything has been

affected by sin. Suffering is the common lot of humanity resulting from disease and accident, or the movement of tectonic plates. It can also be a consequence of sin, our own or others'. Another form of suffering comes from those who hate any who stand on God's truth. As Christians, we have been warned to expect such suffering.[33] How we react is often a very powerful witness to others.

God created men and women with free choice. Not only does this mean that he may not intervene to protect us from the consequences of our wrong choices, but neither will he necessarily intervene to prevent the consequences of our sin affecting the innocent. In many instances, God has brought good out of intolerable situations. To someone in pain it is not always helpful to talk of the benefits which can result from suffering, but they do exist.

i   C S Lewis talks of pain as the megaphone God uses to attract our attention. We often cry out to God only at the end of our tether. Many hurting people in Rwanda have first begun to believe in God because of their anguish. Many falsely accused prisoners have found God in prison and were enabled to bring other prisoners to faith. They would echo the Psalmist who said, "It is good for me that I have been afflicted, that I may learn your statutes."[34]

ii "In this you greatly rejoice, though now for a little while, if need be, you have been grieved by various trials, that the genuineness of your faith, being much more precious than gold that perishes, though it is tested by fire, may be found to praise, honour and glory at the revelation of Jesus Christ."[35] Often, in times of deep trouble our faith emerges stronger than before as we experience the presence of God in our difficulties. Many Rwandan Christians came through the genocide with faith much stronger and more dynamic; they had proved their faith in the fire.

iii "My brethren, count it all joy when you fall into various trials, knowing that the testing of your faith produces
patience."[36] Not only our faith, but our endurance and
patience, are tested in the anguish of suffering. We discover
what is truly important. 1 Peter 5:10 assures us of God's
presence with us in our pain, and that he will strengthen us
through it.

iv "If you should suffer for righteousness' sake, you are
blessed."[37] George,[38] a Christian leader who had been
released after two years in prison, having been falsely
accused, said, "They were the most wonderful two years of
my life. I saw people coming to faith daily." God had truly
blessed him in that time.

v Romans 8:17–18 and 1 Peter 4:12–14 both speak of sharing the suffering of Christ, so that we can in some way glorify him and indeed share in his glory.

vi 2 Corinthians 1:3–4 describes how our suffering can be a
benefit to others as we comfort them with the comfort we
have ourselves received from God. Soon after I started
work in parish ministry, I became depressed. Some months
later, when I returned to work, I met a friend who had
recently had a baby and was suffering from post-natal
depression. She would burst into tears at the least excuse. I
said, "I was like that a few months ago." "Oh Meg," she
cried. "How wonderful to speak with someone who under-
stands how I feel!" I thanked God that he had been able to
use my suffering in that way. I still would rather not have
gone through that time, but was glad it could be used.

Rosa was a Hutu who had the misfortune to look more like a
Tutsi. In April 1994, she was living in Kigali with her husband
and five children, and had recently found herself pregnant

again. When the carnage started, she was nearly killed by one of the gangs. She fled to a Hutu friend for protection. After the war, she was falsely accused of involvement in the slaughter and imprisoned in January 1995, with her small baby who died soon afterwards. She became deeply depressed, living only for visits from her husband. She began to hate both the Hutu who had tried to kill her and the Tutsi who had imprisoned her. "I thought that God had left me," she said. "I had become a believer in 1992, but this made me think deeper about God. Why have you allowed this? Why did you make me neither Hutu nor Tutsi, so that I am persecuted by both sides? God comforted me, showing me that although I could trust no human being, I could trust him as my Parent. I prayed even though my heart ached." In 1997, her husband died. "The children are still small," she cried. "Who will look after them? Who will look after me and visit me? I lost hope and began to despair. I tried to pray, but could only cry."

In May 2001, officials investigated her case. They found no witnesses and no case against her, and in January 2002, she was released by presidential decree. She returned to her husband's home area, where she was reunited with her children. The past few years had been very hard for them, and she found it hard to connect to them. Although she had a house to live in, she had no work, and life was difficult. She started to go to church and found friends to help.

In February 2002, at an AEE seminar at Gikongoro, she realised that the questions they discussed were hers. "Was all that happened to me God's will? I realised that people, not God, had done this. If God is all-powerful, why did he allow what happened to me? If God is truly a God of love, how could he have let my baby die, and my husband, while I was imprisoned? All of those questions were mine."

In the workshop on the cross, she transferred her pain and anger to the Lord Jesus. "I realised that God redeemed pain," she said. "Despite the burdens of poverty and raising my children on my own, I began to believe that Jesus would redeem that pain. I have a burden to pray for this country, so that people will not make bad choices, because the consequences of their choices fall on innocent people. I pray that God will fill people with his love. He has redeemed my sorrow, he has given me friends, he has enabled me to feed and clothe my children. He helps me to go to prisons and tell them what God has done for me and to share my testimony everywhere."

In a country where it is extremely rare for a widow to be remarried, she has found a young man to love her and to be a father to her children. Their wedding, in 2003, was a day of great rejoicing for the Christians in her community.

Many Rwandans, like Rosa, have found their burden of pain not only lifted but also transformed and redeemed. This does not mean that the situation is restored to what it was before, but it can be changed, and good brought out of the suffering. "He can actually turn our tragedies around and redeem them so that we end up better off than if they had never happened. We cannot have our loved ones restored to us in this life, and we may not have material things restored, but in our hearts, we can be in a situation of gain."[39]

Of the many examples of redemptive suffering in the Bible,[40] the one most often used in Rwanda is the story of Joseph, sold into slavery by his brothers. His employer's wife falsely accused him of rape and he was imprisoned for years. He could have thought himself abandoned by God. God did not force the brothers or Potiphar's wife to do evil, but he used their actions to bring good, not only for Joseph himself, but also for the whole nation. God redeemed his suffering, and Joseph was eventually able to say to his brothers, "You meant evil against me but God meant it for good, to bring it about that many people should be kept alive, as they are today."[41]

The Lord Jesus is the ultimate example of redemptive suffering. The agony of the cross, with its attendant shame, pain and rejection, enabled him to redeem suffering humanity.

II "How can a just God allow so much injustice in the world?"
The exiles in Babylon asked this question. Ezekiel replied,
"Yet you say, 'The way of the Lord is not just.' Hear now, O
house of Israel: Is my way not just? Is it not your ways that are
not just?"[42]

The Bible repeatedly says that God loves justice,[43] but
humans often frustrate this justice by our actions.[44] Gary
Haugen[45] challenges Christians to personal involvement.

> As Christians we have learned much about sharing the love of
> Christ with people all over the world who have never heard
> the gospel. We continue to see the salvation message preached
> in the far corners of the earth and to see indigenous Christian
> churches vigorously extending Christ's kingdom on every
> continent. We have learned how to feed the hungry, heal the
> sick and shelter the homeless.
>
> But there is one thing we haven't learned to do, even
> though God's Word repeatedly calls us to the task. We haven't
> learned how to rescue the oppressed. [...] It is perhaps more
> accurate to say that as people committed to the historic faith
> of Christianity, we have *forgotten* how to be such a witness of
> Christ's love, power and justice in the world. In generations
> past the great leaders of Christian Revival in North America
> and Great Britain were consumed by a passion to declare the
> gospel and to manifest Christ's compassion and justice. But
> somewhere during the twentieth century some of us have
> simply stopped *believing* that God can actually use us to answer
> the prayers of children, women and families who suffer under
> the hand of abusive power or authority in their communities.
> We sit in the same paralysis of despair as those who don't even
> claim to know a Saviour – and in some cases, we manifest
> even *less* hope.[46]

Ezekiel 22:25–30 describes the violence and injustice in the
land of Judah. God says, "I sought for a man among them who

would make a wall, and stand in the gap before me on behalf of the land, that I should not destroy it; but I found no one."[47] The anguish in God's heart is almost palpable as he says, "but I found no one". As a result, he brought destruction to Jerusalem and the people were taken into exile. God looked for someone to intervene in situations of injustice, so that he would not have to bring judgement on his people Israel. Isaiah says the same. "Truth is nowhere to be found, and whoever shuns evil becomes a prey. The Lord looked and was displeased that there was no justice. He saw that there was no-one, he was appalled that there was no-one to intervene."[48] He is still look-ing to his people to intervene in times of injustice.

We often ask the God of justice to intervene in situations of injustice, considering that it is his business not ours. Yet he has chosen to work through his church. A Christian, in despair about some injustice, yelled at God at the Grand Canyon, "Where were you?" The echo came back, "Where were you?" Just as people hear the good news of the gospel because peo-ple preach it, or the hungry are fed and the sick are healed because men and women of compassion go in the name of Christ to feed and heal, so victims of injustice are helped because men and women are prepared to intervene, at times even risking their lives.

Had the Rwandan church not kept silent in the face of the assassinations in the months before the genocide, or the injus-tice for the forgotten refugees in Uganda who eventually invaded as the RPF, the horror of the war and the genocide might never have happened. Undoubtedly, God is passionately committed to justice so that humankind should no longer be oppressed; but he has left it to us, his people, to share that commitment, and to confront injustice wherever it is found.

III If God is all powerful why did he not stop the genocide?
Once Rhiannon Lloyd was teaching in an orphanage. She asked the children what God should have done to prevent

their parents' murder. "Should he have struck the killers dead?" she asked. After a short silence: "No, that would have made him no better than the *interahamwe*," they replied. "Should he have paralysed them so that they could not kill?" "If he did, he would have to paralyse all sinners and soon there would be no one left unparalysed!" She was amazed at the spiritual maturity of those suffering youngsters.

When God created humankind he gave us the freedom to choose to obey or disobey. He did not want robots programmed to love and obey him; he wanted people to enjoy a relationship with him, in willing, joyful obedience to his will. Robots would not hurt and wound each other, but neither would they have any freedom to form loving relationships, either between themselves or with God.

> Jesus told us to pray, "Your will be done on earth as it is in heaven" (Matthew 6:10). There is no injustice in heaven, no killing, no suffering. God's will is done there. Jesus wants his will to be done on earth also. If he's asking us to pray for God's will to be done, this means that everything that is happening can't be God's will. When will God's will be done? The prayer says, "Your kingdom come, your will be done." When people submit to God's Kingship, they do his will. When they reject him as King, they don't do his will. Rather they follow their own rebellious hearts.[49]

If God is in control and knows what is going to happen, we imagine it to be his fault for not preventing it. God will never force us to do his will, and he weeps over our wrong choices:

> Oh, that my people would listen to me, that Israel would walk in my ways! (Psalm 81:13)

Oh, that you had heeded my commandments! Then your peace would have been like a river, and your righteousness like the waves of the sea. (Isaiah 48:18)

O Jerusalem, Jerusalem, the one who kills the prophets and stones those who are sent to her! How often I wanted to gather your children together, as a hen gathers her brood under her wings, but you were not willing! (Luke 13:34)

God allows us to suffer the consequences of our own choices, longing that these will drive us back to him. Sadly, others too suffer the consequences of our sin, as many have found in Rwanda.

True forgiveness involves leaving all forms of revenge to God; it involves our will, a decision to forgive; it means facing up to reality, to what actually happened; it may involve forgiving ourselves for our part in the business, or accepting that we were a victim who could not affect what happened, and letting go of false guilt. Above all, we must recognise God's love and justice in the situation and release our desire to blame him. None of this is easy. Indeed it is impossible unless we see how much God has done for us in the great exchange on the cross.

Jonah, that wayward prophet, was successful and respected as a prophet in his own land until God told him to go to Nineveh, the capital of the cruel and aggressive Assyrians. They had already done much damage in Israel, and potentially would do more. Instead of obeying God, he fled to the other end of the known world. Even when he did eventually agree to go to Nineveh, he obviously rejoiced at the message God gave him: "Forty days more, and Nineveh shall be overthrown!"[50] Jonah was furious when the Ninevites repented and sought God's mercy. He considered that they deserved judgement rather than God's mercy.

It is hard to ask God to bless our enemy. Hearing Jonah's

story, Baptiste,[51] a church teacher, stood in tears before his congregation, and confessed his hatred for the Tutsi soldiers who had killed his father and two elder brothers. "For ten years," he said, "I have not wanted to be in the same room as a Tutsi, or to speak to one. Last week, I had to spend a day in Byumba and started talking to a Christian Tutsi. I began to realise that I had been colouring them all the same. Today, I have finally been enabled to relinquish my hatred, and to pray for all Tutsi." Later, he rejoiced that that day ranked with the day he first believed. "I have been released from the load of bitterness I have carried since I was fifteen years old," he said.

However hard it is to ask God to bless our enemies, he calls us to do it. As Baptiste found, when we pray for them, the bitter hurt of resentment often melts away. God may change the hearts of those who wronged us, although that should not affect our willingness to forgive.

In the prisons of Rwanda are many who have found God's forgiveness for terrible acts. Some have admitted their sins before the courts and have been released to spend time in rehabilitation camps. Many others, falsely accused, are now being released for lack of evidence, but, after up to eight years in prison, many are very bitter. They too must learn to forgive.

"Mahatma Ghandi once said that if we all live by an 'eye for an eye' kind of justice, the whole world would be blind. He was right. Reinhold Niebuhr, the theologian, saw this after World War II when he said, 'We must finally be reconciled with our foe, lest we both perish in the vicious circle of hatred.' Forgiveness breaks pain's grip on our minds and opens the door to a new beginning."[52]

Notes

1. See Appendix 2 for the story of Kiramuruzi
2. See chapter 11 for details of the work and teaching of MOUCECORE
3. A potent alcoholic beverage

4. 2 Corinthians 5:19 (RSV)
5. Luke 23:49
6. Quintilian, Epistle 101 to Lucilius
7. Seneca, Dialogue 3:2.2
8. Mark 15:34
9. Isaiah 59:2
10. See chapter 5 for a description of these exchanges
11. 2 Corinthians 2:10–11; Ephesians 4:26–27
12. See chapter 1 for his story
13. Luke 23:34
14. 1 Peter 2:23 (RSV)
15. Romans 12:19
16. Isaiah 53:12b
17. Kendall, 2001, p 27
18. Deuteronomy 32:35–36; Romans 12:19; Hebrews 10:30
19. Luke 6:27–28 (RSV)
20. Monbourquette, 2000, p 34
21. Ibid, p 35
22. See chapter 3 for her story
23. Kendall, 2001, p 26
24. Jonathan Aitken, *Prayers for People under Pressure* (Continuum, London, 2005)
25. 1 Peter 3:9
26. Kendall, 2001, p 26
27. Ibid, pp 35–6
28. Job 2:9, 10
29. Job 42:3, 6
30. Matthew 28:17
31. Although these are some of the questions tackled in the AEE seminars, the treatment is the author's own.
32. C S Lewis, *A Grief Observed*, 1976, p 27
33. eg John 15:18–21
34. Psalm 119:71
35. 1 Peter 1:6–7
36. James 1:2–3
37. 1 Peter 3:14
38. Not his real name
39. Lloyd with Bresser, 2001, p 37
40. eg Job, Naomi, and the promise that God will restore the years that the locust has eaten in Joel 2:23–27

41. Genesis 50:20 (RSV)
42. Ezekiel 18:25 (RSV). See also Ezekiel 33:17
43. eg Psalm 33:5; 37:28; Isaiah 61:8
44. eg Micah 6:8; Ecclesiastes 4:1; James 5:4–7
45. Former director of the UN genocide investigation in Rwanda and now president of International Justice Mission
46. Haugen, 1999, p 72
47. Ezekiel 22:30
48. Isaiah 59:15–16 (NIV)
49. Lloyd with Bresser, 2001, p 31
50. Jonah 3:4 (NRSV)
51. Not his real name
52. Graham, 1991, p 44

CHAPTER FIVE

Transactions at the cross

"For I am not ashamed of the gospel of Christ, for it is the power of God to salvation for everyone who believes, for the Jew first and also for the Greek. For in it the righteousness of God is revealed from faith to faith; as it is written, 'The just shall live by faith.'"

(Romans 1:16–17)

While **forgiveness is central** to the Christian faith, only the power of the cross can enable us to forgive, as Odette found. Most of her family had been killed in the church at Nyamata. Among the bones at the Genocide Museum there, are those of three of her children. In 1994, her husband was working in Kigali, and she had moved there to be with him, leaving her three youngest children with a Hutu neighbour who had promised to look after them. Her oldest child had stayed with an aunt so that she could continue in school. This aunt was married to a Hutu and managed to protect the child. When the fighting started, her husband was killed and Odette fled. She returned to Nyamata as soon as she could, to find that her children had been killed.

After the genocide, she had started looking after orphans in an effort to assuage a pain so deep she could not talk about it; indeed she could hardly talk at all. At the first seminar which Rhiannon led at Nyamata in 1994, Odette had written some of her story down. She did not feel much relief at the time, but later she cried all night and knew that some of the agony was leaving her. She began to be able to talk a little, but still the burden of pain was immense.

Three years later, she attended another seminar where she was in a group with two Hutu. After she had listened to their stories, and heard something of their pain, she began to talk about her time as a refugee. The death of her children was still too painful to mention. It was not until another seminar in 2000, that she accepted that ethnic differences were unimportant. That day, as she nailed her hatred of Hutu to the cross, she was at last free. Only then did she fully realise what Jesus had done for her at Calvary.

She found the Hutu neighbour who had caused the death of her children, and told him she had forgiven him. She said that now she can even love him. She is now looking after eight children, her own and seven orphans, and she is one of the AEE team working for healing and reconciliation in the Nyamata area.

Why is the cross so effective? What happened when Jesus of Nazareth, an obscure carpenter become roving Jewish rabbi, was crucified in a Roman execution? Why is what he did 2,000 years ago still effective for us today?

Throughout the Bible, we read that our sin separates us from God. One of the first actions of Adam and Eve, after they sinned, was to hide from God,[1] and part of his judgement on their sin was to expel them from the Garden where they had freely walked with him.[2] Yet he still wanted a relationship with them. He could not deny their sin, since he is a holy God, but he set about teaching them that sin needs to be covered, the meaning of the Hebrew words *kippurim* or *kaphar*, atonement.

In Leviticus 16 we read how Aaron, and the high priests who followed him, having first entered the Holiest Place of the Tabernacle with the blood of a bull killed for their own sins, were now able to enter, on behalf of the whole people, with the blood of a goat which had been killed for their sins.

This blood was sprinkled seven times over the mercy seat which covered the ark of the covenant, containing the stone tables on which were written the ten commandments. Moses had told the people that God lived above the cherubim, whose wings arched over the mercy seat. The number seven in the Bible is usually a symbol for completeness. The blood was a complete covering for the many times that they had broken God's law during the previous year. Only because it was sprinkled before him was God able to continue in a relationship with his people.

Gila Garaway, a Messianic Jew, concerned for reconciliation in Congo, points out that the English translations of Exodus 25:20–22 obscure the Hebrew. The cherubim are described as being above the mercy seat with their wings outstretched and, "their faces one to another; towards the mercy seat."[3] The Hebrew *ish le achav le kaporet* literally means, "man to his brother to the atonement". Only as man faces his brother with his sin covered can reconciliation begin.

The first chapters of Leviticus, with their emphasis on blood, sound horrible to modern ears, but it is a powerful symbol. It teaches that sin separates us from God, and that a death is necessary before relationship can be restored. The people were forbidden to eat the blood of any animal because "the life of the flesh is in the blood".[4] When the Lord Jesus said that unless they ate of his flesh and drank of his blood they could have no life, most of the Jews listening to him were so revolted by the thought of drinking blood that they turned away from him.[5] The powerful message in his words was that he was offering them his own life in exchange for their sinful lives.

The writer to the Hebrews makes clear that the blood of bulls and goats was not able to remove sin from the people. It merely covered it, enabling God to look again at them, but every sin entailed repetition of the ritual, and every year the blood needed to be sprinkled again on the mercy seat. At the moment Jesus died, the veil separating the Holy Place and the Holiest of all was ripped in two from top to bottom, showing that the way into God's presence was now open to all, through the death of Jesus the Messiah.[6] He, the only true man who had ever lived, had perfectly kept God's law. He was without sin, and was thus able to be the final perfect sacrifice that completely took away our sins.

Not only our sin was dealt with on the cross. In September 1994, on her first visit to Rwanda, Rhiannon Lloyd went to Nyamata. As she listened to the horror of what happened there, and saw the anguish on face after face, the thought crossed her mind, "Only a crucified God is big enough to carry all this pain."[7] She began to see that on the cross, Jesus not only bore our sins but also the sins of the perpetrators, as well as the pain of their victims. Later, reading Derek Prince's book, *Atonement*, she was happy to learn that *avon*, the Hebrew word for iniquity, includes all the consequences of evil.[8]

Max Lucado is another who tells how the Lord Jesus bore the consequences of our sin. In the Bible, he says, thorns are a symbol of the results of sin,[9] and the crown of thorns which was rammed down on Jesus' head was a symbol of the results of our sin.

If the fruit of sin is thorns, isn't the thorny crown on Christ's brow a picture of the fruit of our sin that pierced his heart?

What is the fruit of sin? Step into the briar patch of humanity and feel a few thistles. Shame. Fear. Disgrace. Discouragement. Anxiety. Haven't our hearts been caught in these brambles?

The heart of Jesus, however, had not. He had never been cut by the thorns of sin. What you and I face daily, he never knew. Anxiety? He never worried. Guilt? He was never guilty! Fear? He never left the presence of God! Jesus never knew the fruits of sin ... until he became sin for us.

And when he did, all the emotions of sin tumbled in on him

like shadows in a forest. He felt anxious, guilty and alone. Can't you hear the emotions in his prayer? "My God, my God, why have you rejected me?" (Matt 27:46) These are not the words of a saint. This is the cry of a sinner.[10]

What a joy to realise that Jesus wore that invisible crown of thorns, as well as the visible one, so that we might receive a crown of glory!

Derek Prince describes what he calls the Divine Exchange which took place at the cross. "All the evil due, by justice, to come to us came on Jesus, so that all the good due to Jesus, earned by his sinless obedience, might be made available to us."[11]

He lists nine specific aspects of this exchange:

1 **Jesus was punished that we might be forgiven** (Isaiah 53:4–5; Romans 5:1; Colossians 1:19–22). This is the aspect of the atonement most frequently discussed, to the extent that we often ignore the other exchanges that took place.

2 **Jesus was wounded that we might be healed.** Prince stresses that this means physical healing but it also includes the deep wounds of the heart experienced by many in Rwanda (Isaiah 53:4–5; 1 Peter 2:24).

3 **Jesus was made sin with our sinfulness that we might be righteous with his righteousness** (Isaiah 53:10; 2 Corinthians 5:21; Isaiah 61:10). Many Christians have never realised that they can be clothed in the perfect righteousness of Jesus rather than the filthy rags of our own attempts at righteousness (Isaiah 64:6).

4 **Jesus died our death that we might share his life** (Romans 6:23; Hebrews 2:9). John 10:10 tells us that Jesus wants us to experience life in all its fulness.

5 **Jesus was made a curse that we might receive the blessing** (Galatians 3:13–14). This is especially relevant

in a country like Rwanda, and indeed most of Africa, where traditional religion teaches the dangers of incurring a curse by failure to appease the spirits.

6   **Jesus endured our poverty that we might share his abundance** (2 Corinthians 8:9). Prince stresses that God wants everyone to receive the blessing that comes from giving. Rather than speak about riches, he uses abundance, believing that God wants everyone to have an abundance of this world's riches in order that they may give to others. He does not accept that God wants every Christian to be prosperous, as taught by the Prosperity Gospel proponents. On the contrary, God's desire is that we may have an "abundance for every good work" (2 Corinthians 9:8).

7   **Jesus bore our shame that we might share his glory** (Psalm 69:7; Hebrews 12:2; 2:10). On the cross, Jesus hung naked, his shame exposed. Countless rape victims in Rwanda have rejoiced to realise that Jesus bore their shame and wants them covered in his glory.

8   **Jesus endured our rejection that we might enjoy his acceptance** (Isaiah 53:3; Psalm 69:8; Matthew 27:46; Ephesians 1:5–6). He was rejected by his enemies, his friends deserted him, Peter denied him and at the end, he even felt rejected by God, all so that we might be received into the family of God with all its privileges.

9   **Our old man died in Jesus that the new man might live in us.** Prince says that Jesus was both the last Adam, destined to destruction and the second Man destined to life (1 Corinthians 15:45–49). In him we become a new creation (2 Corinthians 5:17).[12]

One more exchange is illustrated by many Christians in Rwanda:

10   **He endured our sorrow that we might have his joy** (Isaiah 53:3; John 15:11).

These exchanges at the cross have become a meaningful reality to many Christians in Rwanda. Through the Healing and Reconciliation seminars for Christian leaders organised by AEE and initially run by Dr Rhiannon Lloyd, thousands have nailed their pain and anger to a large wooden cross in a symbolic action, and have received in exchange joy and peace as they have forgiven unspeakable harm.

In 1994, Rhiannon was invited by MedAir, a Christian relief organisation, to work with Christians in Nyamata. As she was flying into Kigali, thinking about the traumatised people she would be meeting, and praying about her role, she felt God saying that it was not her medical abilities, or her psychiatry, that would help in this situation. "There is only one thing powerful enough to heal this nation, and that is the cross of my Son," he said. She arrived in Rwanda knowing only one thing for certain. Whatever she did, the cross of Jesus Christ had to be central.

MedAir had provided an interpreter, Thaddée, and arranged various meetings for her, mainly in Nyamata. During the next few years, Rhiannon made several visits to Rwanda and visited all the key towns in the country. Over time, the format of the seminars took shape. They start with Rhiannon explaining her own experiences of ethnic hatred, as a Welsh child brought up to hate the English for what they had done in her country. She tells how she had been helped by an English woman who apologised to her for the sins of the English, and enabled her to release her hatred. They explore the roots of bitterness and prejudice which lay behind the slaughter of 1994 in Rwanda.[13] They follow this by looking at some common misunderstandings about the nature of God and consider his character as our loving heavenly Father.

The Cross Workshop is at the heart of the seminars. Just as God often used acted parables when he spoke to his people through the prophets, so the participants now act out what happened at the cross. First the leader asks God to bring back memories of pain, often hidden deep in people's hearts. Each participant writes down their worst memories. These papers are not seen by anyone else but it is important that specific memories of things seen, heard, felt or even dreamed should be mentioned.

An important element of this workshop is listening to stories, in groups of three or four people, mixing as far as possible ethnicity and denominations. As they share their stories, barriers come down as they realise that others, whom they had seen as causing their own pain, also have painful stories. This session takes at least an hour. It is often hard to convince people to share their stories across ethnic barriers, but it is even harder to persuade them to stop.

Feedback of the painful experiences is written on a large wall chart. The symbol of a large red cross is drawn across the wall chart, and the participants are encouraged to tell Jesus, in their own words, about their pain, and to hand it to him.

Following this, a hammer and nails are provided beside a large wooden cross, and each participant is encouraged to nail his or her piece of paper to the cross. When all are done, the cross is taken outside, and the papers removed and burned. As the smoke goes up, they are told to believe that their pain has indeed been received into the heart of God, and that beauty can rise out of those ashes.[14] They are encouraged to pray for those standing on each side of them.

Back in the seminar room, participants are asked to share any evidence, which had often been obscured by their pain, that God had been with them in the midst of their trials. These good memories, listed on another wall chart, give rise to spontaneous praise and worship that goes on as long as time permits – and often far into the night after the official workshop is over.

This good list is often longer than the list of pain:

"I saw a Hutu hide a Tutsi in his home."

"I saw a diabetic running through the marshes with no

insulin, crying out to God for help and he was healed." (For some reason, once the fighting was over, and insulin was again obtainable, the diabetes returned.)

"I came to real faith experiencing God's protection."

"God answered my prayers and I miraculously escaped."

"I lost everything I possessed but discovered what was really of value in life."

They end this session by reading John 1:5, "The light shines in the darkness, and the darkness did not overcome it." "Do you see how this verse has been proved to be true in your own experience?" the leaders ask, and a shout of praise goes up.

The next day is like resurrection morning, and only now is forgiveness mentioned, frequently by those who have been released from their pain. The leaders often say, "What has happened? You seem like different people from yesterday. Does anyone want to tell us what has changed?" A long queue usually forms and the stories go on half the morning:

"Something amazing happened in my heart when I nailed my paper to the cross. As I returned to my seat, I felt free to forgive."

"Yesterday morning, I hated those people in the refugee camp which we can see from here, because they killed my family, but this morning I want to bless them. Is there any way you can do this seminar there so that they can be healed like us?"

"As I was nailing my paper to the cross, I was aware that I was nailing someone else's sin against my family. Nailing my sin to the same cross has brought me mercy; in nailing their sin they too will receive mercy."

"This morning our hearts are full of joy because last night we were enabled to forgive. You told us to put our pain on the cross and we did. It is hard to forgive when your heart is full of pain but when we are free of pain we can forgive."

At an orphanage in Butare some three years after the genocide, the children were encouraged to draw some pictures about what they had seen. Suddenly one of the children started wailing. Soon the whole room was in an uproar, as one after another they started weeping and crying out. As a psychiatrist, Rhiannon was horrified. "What have I done?" she asked herself. "How can I help these children who have brought their pain to the light like this?" Turning to the staff she asked if the children had ever had the opportunity to face their pain before. "No," she was told, "they never speak about what happened." She asked the team to go through the room, holding the crying children and to speak words of peace to them. When all was still again, she explained that they could transfer their pain onto Jesus, and described how they could nail their papers to the cross. As they nailed their pictures of horror to the large wooden cross, one child started singing, "*Ku ngoma, ku ngoma, Umwami Yesu ari ku ngoma.*" "On the throne, on the throne, the Lord Jesus is on the throne." The verse goes on, "On the cross he conquered, he has swallowed death completely, the Lord Jesus is on the throne." Soon the children were singing, their faces transformed. About two weeks later, Rhiannon again visited that orphanage. As soon as they saw her, the children started singing the same song. Their hearts had begun to be healed, but they would continue to need help for some time to come.

The final element of the seminar is when the leaders accept the sins of their own ethnic group and stand in the gap,[15] asking forgiveness on behalf of their own people. At the first seminar in 1994, an angry woman had accused Rhiannon, as a white, of having caused Rwanda's problems in the first place. At that stage, Rhiannon had known very little about the history of Rwanda. Her interpreter, Thaddée, briefly described how the Belgians had favoured the Tutsi above the Hutu but had switched allegiance when the revolution was brewing, and favoured the Hutu above the Tutsi, leaving them in the lurch when the revolution happened. The identity cards the Belgians issued had emphasised the divisions between the ethnic groups. In tears, Rhiannon had turned to the woman and asked for forgiveness on behalf of Europeans. The woman had been taken aback and totally disarmed.

Rhiannon realised that she needed to stand in the gap on behalf of whites, for what they had done, not only in Rwanda, but in the whole of Africa, starting with the slave trade. During later seminars, a Tutsi would ask for forgiveness for the sins of the monarchy and the arrogance of Tutsi towards Hutu, and would be hugged by a Hutu participant in forgiveness. A Hutu would then ask for forgiveness on behalf of his people for the marginalisation of Tutsi since 1959, and for the horror of the genocide, and in his turn he would be forgiven. They have found that somehow this releases others in the seminars to seek forgiveness for their own sins. Together with the Cross Workshop, this is the most effective part of the seminar, enabling people to forgive across ethnic barriers.

In 1995 MedAir, who first invited Rhiannon and under whose auspices the first seminars had taken place, had to leave Rwanda. As Rhiannon was wondering what to do next, Antoine Rutayisire invited her to train trauma counsellors for AEE. She felt that the priority was for church leaders to be healed of their pain, and in the seminars which eventually resulted, this was what happened. As a result of their own healing, they were able to face the pain in their congregations and help them find healing.

After that first visit, Thaddée, whose vision it was to visit every major town in Rwanda with these seminars, sadly had to leave for family reasons. A year later Rhiannon's next interpreter had to leave suddenly, and Anastase Sabamungu stepped into the breach. He was a Tutsi who had grown up in exile in Uganda, but had often visited his relatives in Rwanda. He had been pastoring a church in Uganda when the genocide began. After it was over, both he and his wife felt called to go to Rwanda to focus on young people, who had seen such atrocities. They are the future of Rwanda and it seemed essential that their attitudes needed to be healed and changed. At the first seminar he attended as the interpreter, Anastase was himself healed of a burden of pain. He saw the potential for this work and continued as Rhiannon's interpreter whenever she came from the UK. In 1997, she handed to him her role as main facilitator in these seminars. For a time he attempted to carry both jobs but the strain became too much. In 2000, believing that God was calling him to return to his original vision, he handed over the leadership of the seminars to Joseph Nyamutera, a Hutu from Gisenyi. Anastase now works part-time with the seminars and continues to pastor a church.

Joseph was teaching English in a high school in Gisenyi when the genocide began. He went into hiding, so that he would not be forced to kill. When the RPF gained control of Kigali, there was a mass exodus of Hutu, terrified of the reprisals they were sure the Tutsi would exact. Joseph and his family joined the stream of refugees to Goma. Like many others, he lost several members of his family to cholera in the terrible conditions of the camp. During those awful months, he met with God in a new way and became actively involved with Christian work there. At the end of 1996, he returned with the other refugees and tried to resume his life. Early next year he attended an AEE seminar where he was healed of his pain. Rhiannon and Anastase were impressed by his testimony and invited him to a training seminar in Kigali. After praying about it, they both felt that he was the needed Hutu for their team and asked him to join them. Together with Anastase, and Rhiannon when she has been in the country, he has travelled throughout Rwanda demonstrating the power of the cross to transform relationships and to bring healing, forgiveness and reconciliation. In 2000, he took over full leadership of the seminars and now heads up the Evangelism Department of AEE, Rwanda, of which the Healing and Reconciliation Department is part.

By now, there have been literally thousands of people who say that seeing their pain transferred to Jesus on the cross, and hearing people of the other group confess their own sins, has set them free to forgive. Many of the Christian leaders in Rwanda have attended these seminars, and other Christian organisations have a similar session on the cross as part of their teaching, so effective has it been found in the process of healing and forgiveness.

Youth with a Mission, who have a large programme helping the victims of HIV/AIDS, introduce a large wooden cross at the start of their three-day workshop, with a basket of bread below it. As people nail to the cross pieces of paper, on which are written their worries of sickness, debt, school fees etc, they are encouraged to take a piece of bread as a symbol of the broken body of Christ, which they receive in exchange for their broken lives. They find this often brings release from anxiety. Frequently church leaders realise that they have been judgemental in their attitudes to AIDS victims and have failed to visit them. These wrong attitudes are nailed to the cross in penitence and the bread of forgiveness received in their place.

Sometimes when an AIDS orphan tells his or her story there is a spontaneous repentance to the child, with men kneeling before him on behalf of Dads who have brought the killer disease into the family. At the end of the workshop, the cross is covered with pieces of paper and the group gathers outside to burn the papers and praise God.

The burning of papers is followed by breaking of bread and passing round the wine (or rather, herb tea) and reading out the passages where the Lord asked us to remember what his death signifies. The exchange showed that with repentance the Lord gives his cleansing and his broken bread to resource them for all the broken situations they are returning to. It was the first time different denominations had broken bread together and there was much joy and also a window opening that maybe we could remember the Lord's supper more than once a month in church.

It is difficult to measure the effectiveness of this but we feel that in relation to AIDS which is a disease of the blood, the Lord is wanting us to remember in higher profile what his blood achieved and goes on achieving.[16]

Notes

1. Genesis 3:8
2. Genesis 3:24
3. Exodus 25:20 (RSV)
4. Leviticus 17:11a
5. John 6:53–66
6. See Hebrews 10:19–22
7. Personal conversation with the author. All other unattributed quotations are also from such personal conversations
8. Prince, 2000, p 35
9. See eg Genesis 3:17–18; Numbers 33:55; Proverbs 22:5; Matthew 7:16
10. Lucado, 2000, p 26
11. Prince, 2000, p 37
12. List, ibid, p 31. Comments and relevant references added by the author
13. See chapter 2
14. Isaiah 61:3
15. See chapter 6 for a fuller discussion of this concept, taken from Ezekiel 22:30
16. Account given by Richard and Prilla Rowland, who used to be missionaries in Rwanda, and who come back once or twice a year to conduct these workshops

CHAPTER SIX

Standing in the gap

"So I sought for a man among them who would make a wall, and stand in the gap before me on behalf of the land, that I should not destroy it; but I found no one." *(Ezekiel 22:30)*

If listening to each other's stories is important, and nailing their pain to the cross releasing, the final element of the AEE seminars, standing in the gap, is also extremely effective. Gilbert was born to a Tutsi family and brought up Roman Catholic. He was 20 years old and on holiday from the Roman Catholic secondary school in the Nyamata District when the war started in 1994. When the killers came, he and his family fled. He was separated from the rest of the family, but returned to his home in the afternoon, where he found his sister, who had been beaten with a club with nails in it and cut by a machete. He did what he could to help, but she was so severely injured that she did not know him. The next day, the killers came back and he had to run, leaving her. When he returned a few days later, he found that she had been beaten again and had died. A week later, his mother was killed, together with his grandmother, and another sister with her children who had all hidden in the church. He went there that same evening, and was horrified and frightened by the number of bodies he saw. With other dazed survivors, he did what he could to help the wounded and to bury the dead, but again the killers came. This time he fled to the nearby swamp, where he hid in the water for three weeks until the RPF arrived.

Subsequently, as part of a university social science course, he did a placement with AEE because he was interested in their Reconciliation programme. When he first saw Joseph, he wondered how he, as a Hutu, could possibly be an agent of reconciliation. How could he go to an area like Nyamata, where so many Tutsi had been killed? When he knew him better, he realised that Joseph was a good man, even though he was Hutu. Gilbert listened as people shared testimonies of how they had been helped in an AEE seminar. Realising how many had been released from hatred, he determined to go to one to find for himself what they had found. As a Christian, he knew that he had to forgive and thought he had done so; but, as they shared their stories a few weeks later, he realised that he had not understood the full meaning of forgiveness. A Hutu standing in the gap released him to forgive truly. To hear a Hutu speaking of the horrors and willing to accept the blame, even though he had done none of it, helped Gilbert to release his anger. This is why he too likes to go with the team and stand in the gap on behalf of Tutsi, especially in Hutu areas like Ruhengeri and Byumba, where many acts of vengeance took place following the genocide. Having now heard the stories of many Hutu, he realises their pain, where before he had only seen his own. As he shares his story in Hutu areas, they weep with him for his pain. Gilbert is now doing workshops on bereavement with World Vision. Hearing painful stories across ethnic divides helps the Hutu and Tutsi alike to have compassion for each other.

The phrase "standing in the gap" is taken from Ezekiel 22:30. God had looked at the unrighteousness amongst his people of Judah; leadership was corrupt (22:25, 27); the priests were profaning the worship of the Temple (22:26); the prophets were speaking outright lies (22:28); and the people were generally corrupt and greedy, oppressing the poor and needy (22:29). God says, "So I sought for a man among them who would make a wall, and stand in the gap before me on behalf of the land, that I should not destroy it, but I found no one."[1] As a result the land was destroyed and the people taken into captivity for 70 years. This suggests that if only one person had been acting in a priestly way, interceding on behalf of his people, God would not have destroyed the land.

Nothing in what follows detracts from the need to confess our own attitudes, thoughts and actions. We must take responsibility for our own sins, but "the Bible talks about collective as well as individual responsibility, of corporate as well as personal guilt. For corporate guilt, there is another kind of repentance which can also be very powerful in bringing about healing and reconciliation. It is called Identificational Repentance."[2] This is what the AEE team calls "standing in the gap". When an individual has sinned against us and confesses that sin, it is much easier to forgive. So, too, if an individual stands on behalf of his people and confesses their sin, it is much easier to forgive those people.

Sin has created a vast divide between God and humankind; it is called alienation, since all sin breaks the fellowship we were intended to have with God. We are sinners, not only because we commit wrongful acts or thoughts, but also because we inherit a sinful nature. When our Lord Jesus became sin for us on the cross, he hung in the gap between a holy God and sinful, rebellious humanity, making it possible for us to enter once more into fellowship with God. Only he could do it because he was without sin. If we are in him, we are clothed in his righteousness, and are able to join with him in interceding for our people.

Intercede comes from the Latin word *intercedere*, and is formed from two words, *inter*, between, and *cedere*, to go. An intercessor is therefore a go-between. When we intercede, we are placing ourselves between the person or people for whom we are praying and the wrath of God towards their sin, or between a person and the object of his or her wrath. When Nabal offended David, the king threatened to destroy the whole family. Abigail stood in the gap on her husband's behalf, saying, "Upon me alone, my lord, be the guilt ... "[3] David had been insulted and his instinctive reaction, as is so often the case, was to take his revenge on the whole family. In the same way, we seek someone to blame for our hurt, and all the people linked to the one who caused our pain become tarred with the same brush. So, "Hutu killed my family" is the reaction, regardless of the fact that the actual killer might be dead. "Tutsi raped my sister", even if the RPF soldier concerned might himself have been Hutu. When we stand in the gap, we must be prepared to take that blame, and anything else that the injured parties want to hurl at the perpetrators, as Abigail did.

At a meeting in Kigali soon after the genocide, a South African pastor told how a group of clergy in Cape Town were praying that God would intervene to stop some fighting taking place between two rival groups in the days before the 1994 election there. As they prayed, they heard the Holy Spirit tell them to go and stand between the groups who were shooting at each other. "But we might be killed!" they said. No reply came, except the reiteration that they should stand between them. In much trepidation, with no assurance that they would not be killed, they obeyed – and the fighting stopped!

"The greatest wounding against mankind is the result of sins committed by a corporate body – governments, institutions, churches, etc., – not by individuals. The problem is that even though we are part of the corporate body, we tend to excuse ourselves from taking personal responsibility. The sins then are never owned and confessed."[4] Even though we may be part of those bodies, often we have no say in what is done on our behalf, and frequently we are unaware of the effects. Because it is at a remove, we do not feel personally involved and so these wounds are never acknowledged, and the sins never confessed.

Unless someone identifies themselves with the corporate body who perpetrated the sins and confesses them, the sins remain unconfessed. These become like festering wounds in the victims who cry out for justice to be done. A festering wound in one part of the body eventually poisons the whole body. As these memories linger, bitterness deepens and multiplies often resulting in judgements, increasing resentment, hatred and anger as it is passed down from generation to generation.[5]

How do we deal with these wounds? "Those who have died can't repent of their sins, the ungodly won't, but we as Christians can confess our corporate sin and ask for forgiveness."[6] We are part of a royal priesthood,[7] and like Aaron and Moses of old, we are expected to stand before God on behalf of our people. To be effective, we must be part of the offending group. There is no point in identifying with a group with which we have no connection, just as we cannot as individuals confess the sins of another person.

> Each one of us is responsible for the sins of our own nation and we are not exempt, no matter how virtuous we think we are, from the judgement of our nation as we all share in the tribal group stories that have gone into the shaping of us. Walter Wink quotes, in support of this idea, the example of Martin Niemoller who spent eight years in a Nazi jail for his opposition to Hitler's policies. He was nonetheless the first to say about German atrocities during the Second World War, "We are all guilty".[8]

Goretti, one of the Byumba diocesan workers, was amazed to hear Joseph confess the atrocities committed by Hutu. "How can he identify with those people?" she thought. "I am righteous, and could never say that I am one with those who did such evil." That night God spoke to her, showing her some of the attitudes of her heart. She might not have killed, but she did not object that others were purging Tutsi for her. The first time she stood in the gap as a Hutu, she wept for their sins.

She said, "I did not realise how we are one, even in the horror." She chose, like Jesus, to be numbered with the transgressors.[9]

Although many initially felt like Goretti, Rwandan thinking is much closer to the Hebrew thought patterns than to Western ideas, in stressing family responsibility for sin. In the West, we tend to follow Greek theology in stressing individual guilt, and find it difficult to accept this priestly role of standing in the gap on behalf of a group of people.

Numbers 16:43–48 gives a very powerful example of Aaron in his priestly role, running with his censor of incense into the midst of the people under God's judgement. "He stood between the dead and the living; so the plague was stopped."[10] In the Bible, incense is a picture of the prayers of God's people. Aaron's action was a form of prayer, or intercession, which halted God's judgement.

Often all members of a group are judged because of the offence of one. For example, a woman who has been raped can hate all men. Dr Richard Rowland, in his work with HIV/AIDS victims, often kneels in tears before women who have been raped, confessing this sin committed by men and asking for forgiveness on behalf of men. Anastase and Joseph do the same in the AEE seminars. They are not accepting the sin of the individual who committed the rape, but they are asking for forgiveness on behalf of all men. It is helpful for wounded people to hear someone put into words, "What was done to you was wrong." Open acknowledgement of the sin helps heal the wounds.

Everard[11] told of how during the genocide his wife and two-and-a-half-year-old child had been killed, and he was severely injured. He said, "I was able to move so that I could hide, and people saved me and hid me. I was an evangelist but I hated Hutu. When a Hutu came into the church, I would accept him because I wanted the church to grow, but I myself had no joy. I went to an AEE seminar where I nailed my pain to the cross, and realised that I had been forgiven. I was even able to forgive the killers of my family. I had anger and hatred in my heart against whites, but when Rhiannon stood in the gap, I was able even to release that hatred. The teaching on standing in the gap helped me to forgive."

Certainly, whites have much to confess in the history of Rwanda and especially during the genocide. The United Nations General in Rwanda at the time, Roméo Dallaire says,

> Several times in this book I have asked the question, "Are we all human, or are some more human than others?" Certainly we in the developed world act in a way that suggests we believe that our lives are worth more than the lives of other citizens of the planet. An American officer felt no shame as he informed me that the lives of 800,000 Rwandans were only worth risking the lives of ten American troops; the Belgians, after losing ten soldiers, insisted that the lives of Rwandans were not worth risking another single Belgian soldier.[12]

Wrong attitudes exhibited by whites towards most people of another skin colour provide much to confess. For instance, much of our wealth came from cheap labour resulting from the African slave trade which led to many broken families and millions of deaths, and the Berlin Conference in 1887 divided Africa between the European powers as if the indigenous inhabitants did not exist. The resulting colonialism, in a pretence of civilising the nations, often destroyed their culture and made them feel inferior.[13] The behaviour of the international community in 1994 did nothing to help Rwandans view the *bazungu* any better.

> I passed by an assembly port where French soldiers were loading expatriates into vehicles. Hundreds of Rwandans had gathered to watch all these white entrepreneurs, NGO staff and their families making their fearful exits, and as I wended my way through the crowd, I saw how aggressively the French

were pushing black Rwandans seeking asylum out of the way. A sense of shame overcame me. The whites who had made their money in Rwanda and who had hired so many Rwandans to be their servants and labourers, were now abandoning them. Self-interest and self-preservation ruled.[14]

That day, once the expatriates had been rescued, the troops pulled out, and 2,000 Rwandans under the protection of the United Nations in a school in Kigali were abandoned to the *interahamwe*. Almost all were slaughtered.[15]

Rhiannon confesses these sins at every seminar she attends. In the early seminars, as Rhiannon stood in the gap on behalf of Europeans, it was as if this set the participants free to accept their own guilt on behalf of their own ethnic groups. This would often spark off a time of repentance between the different groups. Once Anastase and Joseph joined the team and confessed the sins of their groups, this freed people to acknowledge their own individual sins. The time of repentance would then often last for hours.

When we stand in the gap, we are taking that priestly role which God looked for in Ezekiel 22:30. This is what Jesus did at his baptism, when he identified with sinful human beings. John the Baptist was horrified, saying, "I need to be baptized by you, and are you coming to me?"[16] Jesus consented to be identified with his people, accepting the baptism of John "for repentance of sin", so that he could better minister to them. This identification became even more acute on the cross, when, as the only sinless human being who had ever lived, he allowed himself to become sin for us. He accepted the transfer of all the consequences of sin upon himself, so that we could gain all the benefits of his sinless life. Although he was innocent, Isaiah tells us that "he was numbered with the transgressors".[17] As a result, he "is able to save to the uttermost those who come to God through him, since he always lives to make intercession for them".[18]

The Cross Workshop: Participants write down their worst memories, share their stories and are encouraged to tell Jesus about their pain and hand it to him. A hammer and nails are then provided for them to nail their piece of paper to the cross. When all are done, the cross is taken outside and the papers are removed and burnt.

Through the Healing and Reconciliation seminars for Christian leaders, organised by AEE (African Evangelistic Enterprise), thousands have received joy and peace in exchange for their pain and anger. The team (from right to left) includes Joseph Nyamutera (Main Leader); Dr Rhiannon Lloyd (founder); Anastase Sabamungu (Pastor); Rhiannon's assistant and a regional team leader.

Joseph heads up the Evangelism Department of AEE and has full leadership of the seminars. He has travelled throughout Rwanda demonstrating the power of the cross to transform relationships and to bring healing, forgiveness and reconciliation. He can be seen here with his wife and two children.

IMIZI YIMYEMERERE NIMITEKEREREZE

ADAMU
UMUGABANE
IGIHUGU
UBWOKO

IMYIZERE
IBY'UMUNTU YA NY-
UZEMO MU BUZIMA
UMURYANGO (Murugo)

BASOKOKURUZA

A banner used to teach about the roots of prejudice that impact the Rwandan mindset. It illustrates the influence of our heritage from Adam, life experience, country, family, tribe, teaching and ancestors.

Wilberforce was out of the country when the 1994 genocide started. He is pictured here with Celine, his daughter, reburying his wife and three of his children. "All the Tutsi in this neighbourhood were pushed in here," he explained, standing beside the burnt-out skeleton of a house. "Then they set fire to some rubber tyres and pushed them inside. They choked to death. The awful thing is that those who did it were our neighbours, and we knew them well."

Aimable is the local team leader for the AEE Healing and Reconciliation Team at Nyamata where most of his family were killed in one of the worst massacres of 1994. He is pictured here with Rhiannon at the memorial site where the bones of his mother and sisters lie.

John Gakwandi is the founder and Director of Solace Ministries, which he set up in 1996 to support rape victims, widows and orphans.

Michel Kayitaba, one of the founding members and Director of MOUCECORE (The Christian Movement for Evangelism, Counselling and Reconciliation). Having survived the genocide he felt the call of God to strengthen the church and enable it to live as the kingdom of God on earth and to play its part in the healing and transformation of Rwanda.

Julienne Kayijuka is the Director of Women's Work for PHARP (Peace-building, Healing and Reconciliation Programme). They run training seminars and teach on subjects such as: Help for traumatised people; Peace-building and conflict resolution; Justice; Righteousness and holy living; Reconciliation; Care for AIDS victims and prevention of HIV/AIDS.

Antoine Rutayisire is the Rwandan Team Leader for AEE. He is pictured here outside the AEE Guest House, named after his predecessor and close friend Israel Havugimana who was killed on the first day of the genocide.

Juliette, an employee of AEE, lost her husband, father, mother, sisters and brothers during the genocide. Until her pain had been addressed she was unable to forgive, but ultimately saw that Jesus had died to give her joy and healing. In this way she was set free to forgive.

Venantie is the wife of a pastor; both are Hutu. Seventeen members of her family were massacred by the invading, mainly Tutsi, army, the RPF. At a seminar run by PHARP Venantie was able to let go of her anger and start to forgive.

Kiramuruzi was the scene of terrible massacres. When Stephanie (left), a Hutu, and her family were captured by the RPF, both her husband and father were killed and their possessions stolen. Agnes (middle), a Tutsi, lost her husband and one of her sons and, at first, could not even look at a Hutu without fear. Here they are with their pastor outside their church.

Edith lost her husband, several children and her aunt during the genocide. She is standing by their grave with Tito, the man who confessed to killing her aunt after a gang of killers forced him to beat her with a club.

Marie Goretti, a Hutu, had repressed her anger against her father after he had tried to kill her when he found that she had been sheltering Tutsi children. This scared her and she began to distrust all men. At a PHARP seminar she started out on the road to forgiveness. She now works as a communications officer for MOUCECORE.

Other biblical examples of people standing in the gap before God on behalf of others include:[19]

Moses	When God said that he would blot out the people and make a new start with Moses, Moses interceded for the people, saying that this would not be in accordance with God's character and would bring disrepute on his name, pleading with him not to destroy them. His plea changed God's mind. (Psalm 106:23; Exodus 32:1–14)
Daniel	He is called "highly esteemed" and "greatly beloved" by God. Yet he prayed for his people saying, "We have sinned and done wrong. We have been wicked and have rebelled; we have turned away from your commands and laws. We have not listened to your servants the prophets."[20] Daniel had not been born when the evil which brought God's judgement on Judah was committed. He was only a boy when taken captive to Babylon; yet he prayed for his people, as one of them. His prayer ends with a moving plea. "O Lord, hear! O Lord, forgive! O Lord, listen and act! Do not delay for your own sake, my God, for your city and your people are called by your name."[21] Like many other people of God in the Old Testament, Daniel bases his prayer on the character and glory of God, not on the merits of his people.
Nehemiah	Twice Nehemiah identifies with the sins his people committed in Israel, before he was born in Susa, the Persian capital. The first time is when he hears that the walls of Jerusalem have been destroyed. He confesses the sins of the people "… which we have sinned against you. Both, I and

my family have sinned. We have offended you deeply ... "[22] Once the walls have been built, he leads the people to renew the covenant with their God, but first leads them in a prayer of confession, again identifying with the sins of the people from the time they left Egypt.[23]

Ezra

A contemporary of Nehemiah, Ezra came from Babylon to restore the beauty and significance of temple worship. He was a teacher of the law of God, an expert in it. He, too, identified with the sins of his people when he says, "O my God, I am too ashamed and humiliated to lift up my face to you, my God; for our iniquities have risen higher than our heads, and our guilt has grown up to the heavens ... "[24]

These are all individuals who identified with the sins of others in order to seek forgiveness and bring healing in their different situations.

Many Christians in America are seeking to stand in the gap and confess the sins of white Americans against indigenous Americans, or African Americans, and barriers are beginning to come down as a result. British Christians are beginning to accept responsibility for the evils of the slave trade and colonialism. European nations are considering a gathering in Berlin to seek the forgiveness of the African nations that were arrogantly carved up for Europe at the Conference of Berlin in 1884. These and many other initiatives are happening because Christians are waking up to the sins committed on their behalf by governments or other institutions. We still do not intercede effectively for our governments to prevent inappropriate legislation.

Walter Wink tells the story of how, in 1986, the United Church of Canada formally apologised for past wrongs committed on the native peoples of Canada by the church, who imposed their civilisation on them in the name of the gospel of Jesus Christ. At the time the tribal elders present showed great joy, but two years later at the next Council meeting, the tribal elders acknowledged the apology without accepting it. They said the wounds were too deep for mere words to heal.

> Rather than a damper or rejection, this "acknowledgement without acceptance" served as the basis for greater dignity and autonomy for Native Americans in the United Church. The genuine contrition of the white majority meant that both sides now recognised the need for healing, and that there would be no "healing lightly" (Jer 6:14), but rather a long process of deliberate restitution and consciousness-raising. In this case, then, acknowledgement but non-acceptance provided the foundation for the process of reconciliation.[25]

Care needs to be taken how we stand in the gap. Native Canadians sometimes say that they do not want apologies that only serve to assuage the guilt of whites. "We have problems enough of our own," they say, "without taking on board your problems as well."

Not only is standing in the gap on behalf of institutions or governments effective, but Anastase or Joseph will stand in the gap on behalf of fathers who have abused their children, or as men seeking forgiveness from women who have been raped; Rhiannon has stood on behalf of doctors or as a woman on behalf of mothers. I have found myself confessing the attitudes of superiority of missionaries towards their converts in the early days in Africa, which left them with such a sense of inferiority.

When individuals stand in the gap:[26]

- They accept that they are members of the same people group who have deeply wounded another group. They do not condone what was done, nor pretend they did this evil if they did not, but they acknowledge that they were capable of it.

- They spell out some of the wrongs done by their people group, acknowledging the hurts experienced by the others.
- They deeply regret what was done to the other group, and ask forgiveness on behalf of their own people, crying out for God's mercy.
- They commit themselves to living in a new spirit for the future.
- It does not mean that those who have actually committed the sins they are confessing are absolved from their acts, or from the consequences of their acts.
- It does not mean that criminals can avoid punishment so that justice is not done.
- It does not mean that those standing in the gap are there in some official capacity. They are exercising the priestly role of interceding for their people.

Individuals must still confess before God their own sins in order to receive forgiveness; but when someone stands in the gap, it can help those who have heard the confession let go of their hatred and bitterness, find the grace to forgive and receive the healing they need from the Holy Spirit.

"Confession, repentance and reconciliation must become a way of life. We, as Christians representing the local church, are God's hope for healing the nation and have a chance to live out these principles in a unique way. It is God's plan that his church and his people adopt this way of life and become priestly reconcilers to hurting people."[27]

We must be prepared to stand in the gap wherever we meet people who have been injured because of actions taken by our own people group, government, church or other institution, even if we did not agree with the action taken. It is a tremendous privilege to see the Holy Spirit remove barriers as we do so, but it can be very costly. Many of those who have stood in the gap have been abused by their own people or families, who see it as a betrayal of their group. Some have even received death threats.

In 1996 in Detmold, Germany, a group of Rwandans from several Christian denominations met together to discuss ways of seeking reconciliation. Some had come over from Rwanda, and Rhiannon was one of the speakers, sharing about the healing seminars she had been conducting in Rwanda. One day she spoke about the theology of standing in the gap. As a white person, she confessed the sins of Europeans in Africa, and specifically in Rwanda. Next day, a Hutu, who had come over from Rwanda, wept as he confessed the sins of Hutu in the genocide. A Tutsi survivor hugged him in forgiveness. The chairman separated them into three groups: Tutsi, Hutu and *bazungu*, for a time of sharing. Each was to seek the guidance of the Holy Spirit as to what they felt they could confess on behalf of their own people group.

The resulting Declaration of Detmold created a storm, both in Europe and in Rwanda. Many were furious with the signatories. "Who gave you the right to say that on our behalf?" they were asked. Some of the signatories received hate mail and even death threats. A year later they met again. They agreed that they had been led by the Holy Spirit to sign the Declaration, and they stood by what they had signed. Standing in the gap means being numbered with the transgressors, so opposition or rejection, even from fellow Christians, is not surprising. The healing results are worth the pain.

At a meeting in a beautiful spot below the Virunga mountains, after a seminar with church leaders to explain to local people what they had been learning, I stood as a white to stand in the gap. I found myself weeping as I felt something of the pain in the heart of God. I confessed the indifference of whites who pass the people daily on the way to visit the gorillas in the mountains. I confessed the attitudes of many of the early missionaries who had considered themselves superior to them. Finally I confessed the divisions brought in by the Belgians when they introduced the identity cards which were the cause of many deaths in the genocide. As I finished, one old lady from the village, with a drawn face, came up and was the first to hug me. "I forgive you," she said. I have no idea who she was, but her face lives with me.

Notes

1. Ezekiel 22:30
2. Lloyd with Bresser, 2001, p 83
3. 1 Samuel 25:24 (RSV)
4. Lloyd with Bresser, 2001, p 84
5. Ibid
6. Ibid, p 85
7. 1 Peter 2:9
8. Parker, p 191
9. Isaiah 53:12
10. Numbers 16:48
11. Not his real name
12. Dallaire, 2003, p 522
13. See chapter 2 for a fuller treatment of this subject
14. Dallaire, 2003, p 286
15. Ibid, p 289
16. Matthew 3:14
17. Isaiah 53:12
18. Hebrews 7:25
19. List is taken from Lloyd with Bresser, 2001, p 86, with comments by the author
20. Daniel 9:5–6a (NIV)
21. Daniel 9:19
22. Nehemiah 1:6b–7a (NRSV)
23. Nehemiah 9:2–36
24. Ezra 9:6
25. Wink, 1998, pp 55–6
26. Adapted from Lloyd with Bresser, 2001, p 86
27. Guillebaud, 2002, p 323, quoting Rhiannon Lloyd

CHAPTER SEVEN

Forgiveness and the law

"Let every person be subject to the governing
authorities; for there is no authority except from
God, and those authorities that exist have been
instituted by God."   *(Romans 13:1, NRSV)*

The justice system had been totally destroyed
in the horrors of 1994, and an accusation was
enough to have someone imprisoned. People were arrested
on genuine charges, but many innocent people were accused
because someone coveted a job or a field owned by the victim,[1] or because of bitterness.

Margaret[2] is a pastor's wife, whose father was arrested and
accused of involvement in the genocide. He was a nurse in one
of the many hospitals where massacres took place. When the
RPF took control of the country, he refused to flee with the
other staff of the hospital since he had not taken part in the
massacre. He was the only visible member of the hospital
remaining, and was an easy target for a pastor who had lost
many members of his family there. He was accused of involvement in the genocide, and imprisoned. Margaret would go
regularly to visit her father in the cramped conditions of the
jail, and went daily when his case came up for trial. One of the
judges actually told her that he knew that the accuser had no
real evidence, and asked if she was not angry with him. "No,"
she replied, "I can see the pain he is in, and as a Christian, I
forgive him." She was shocked when the court said that her
father was old and wise, and should have been able to prevent
the massacre, and devastated when he was found guilty and

sentenced to life imprisonment. In the only bitter comment I ever heard her make, she said, "If this is the justice we have to expect, may God help our nation."

Six years later, the case was heard on appeal, and he was declared innocent of all crimes, though he still had to stay many months in prison before he was finally released. I heard Margaret tell his story to a friend without mentioning how her father came to be accused. I asked about this. "I have totally forgiven that man," she said. "His part is no longer important to me, so I don't mention it." I asked how she had been able to forgive him.

"I see him quite often," she said. "I know his story, and I realise that he was lashing out at my father from frustration and anger. He lost many members of his family, and is still in great pain. How can I add to it? I greet him whenever I see him, but he refuses to speak to me."

Jealousy was another motive for accusation. Chantal's home was next door to President Habyarimana's. She knew his family and visited them. She had no idea of the problems between ethnic groups until 1990 when the RPF invaded, and reprisals were taken against Tutsi. Even then, the Tutsi in her neighbourhood were treated as showpieces. Whenever the government was accused of massacring or ill-treating Tutsi, the accusers would be shown those living in harmony near the president's home.

Chantal's father died of natural causes in 1991, leaving her mother with nine children and two older stepchildren. Not until Easter Day, four days before the start of the genocide, did Chantal's mother grasp their dangerous position. She was returning from mass at her local church when she was attacked by a band of local thugs yelling that she was a Tutsi spy. She screamed for help, and some of those who had been to church with her came to her aid. She was very shaken, and once home she said to her family, "We will all die."

Still not realising that the danger was countrywide, she

arranged for her children to stay with various relations, in the hope that some would survive. On Thursday 6th April at 8pm, the president's plane was shot down, landing in pieces around her neighbourhood. By 4am all the Tutsi in the area had been killed, together with the Hutu who had worked for them.

On the outskirts of Kigali, staying with relations, Chantal and her relatives were surrounded by soldiers who stole their money and a radio but otherwise left them alone. The family fled to a nearby university site where several foreigners lived, and where they thought they would be safe, but within a few days the foreigners were evacuated. As soon as they left, soldiers and *interahamwe* arrived. The Tutsi were separated from the Hutu, and herded into another house. Two by two, they were ordered outside to be killed. Her aunt was one of the first out, but Chantal was further back in the line. The soldier who had taken their radio recognised her uncle, and pulled him from the line, together with Chantal and several other girls. He took them to his home, where he used the girls, and another woman with a small baby, as his "wives". Chantal and this other woman were kept in a small hut in the compound. She still had a little money, and conspired with Chantal to find a grenade so that they could kill as many as possible before they were themselves killed.

The soldier left them as the battle for Kigali intensified. He never returned, and was presumably killed. They stayed where they were, in constant fear. They heard a rumour that the *interahamwe* were coming for them and when they heard a loud knocking at the door, Chantal peered out. Seeing a soldier's uniform, she cried out in fear, "It's the *interahamwe*!" Her friend fetched the grenade, but before taking any action, she too looked out. It was the RPF, who had come to rescue the Tutsi in the area. They were taken to a safe camp where they survived the war.

After the fighting was over, Chantal returned home. She was horrified by the devastation. Of her large family only two other members survived: her five-year-old brother who had been claimed as her own by a Hutu neighbour, and one step-sister who been protected by her Hutu husband. Chantal found a house that was reasonably intact, and tried to make a home for her brother. She was consumed by hatred, and had the awful fear that she had AIDS or was pregnant. Fortunately, neither was true. Wherever she went, she carried a club for her protection. She began trading with the soldiers to earn a little money, but spent most of it on beer. After a while, she realised that she needed to go back to school if she was ever to find a job. There, she met others from her home area and compared stories. She wanted to injure Hutu in whatever way she could, to relieve some of the anger and pain she felt.

"I saw one Hutu from my neighbourhood. We had been friends before the war. We were both Roman Catholics, attending the same church. His house had survived, and he had his family around him. I was jealous of him and I hated him," she said. With another Tutsi lady from her home area, she decided to report this man to the authorities for taking part in the genocide. "I wasn't there. I didn't know what he had done. I just hated him," she said. They rehearsed their story about how they saw him kill a child, and went to the police. They swore the truth of their statement before a Justice. The man was arrested and imprisoned. Chantal was delighted that a Hutu was hurting.

She was now at the Seventh Day Adventist secondary school. Every evening there was a time of prayer and Bible study. "I was brought up as a Catholic, and had never heard of this," she said. "After a time it began to affect me, but if I tried to pray, I had no peace. I would see the face of Ntanturo, the man I had imprisoned. I began to feel guilty, and knew that I was a sinner. If I had not done that terrible thing I do not think I would ever have accepted that I was a sinner. I resolved to go to confession to assuage the guilt. I wanted to do penance for it." Even so, she had no peace.

At this time, she started to go out with a Christian man. She told him what she had done. He was terrified that if she confessed she would go to prison, or be killed by Hutu. Together they went to a meeting at a Full Gospel church, where for the first time she realised the full horror of her sin. She asked for God's forgiveness, and knew that even if she were to be killed she would go to heaven.

She prayed that God would lead her to a Christian member of Ntanturo's family so that she could confess to him. One day, at a meeting in a Pentecostal church, she saw one of Ntanturo's sons, and knew that he was the one. After the meeting, but before she could say a word, he asked for her forgiveness for his harsh attitudes towards her. "I want to ask your forgiveness for the lies I told," she cried. He told her that he had been praying for her since he had become a Christian, that she too would believe.

To his mother's disgust, he visited Chantal, and together they studied the Bible. She told him of her fears about retracting her statement, and they prayed that she would know the right way forward and the right timing. Eventually , she was able to visit Ntanturo in prison. At first, he was reluctant to see her, as he was sure she had further torments in store, but when they met, she asked his forgiveness for her lies and for the five years he had spent in prison. She told him that she would do what she could to release him.

Court procedures were still painfully slow, and it was another three months before the judicial enquiry. Many Tutsi did their best to dissuade her from appearing as a witness for the defence, but she sat down with Ntanturo's family. By this time she was settled in a new home, with a husband and baby. They worshipped at an Assemblies of God church, whose members prayed for her to tell the truth boldly. The court asked her why she had changed her story, and how they could believe her this time. She told them that she had been convicted by God, and knew that she had to speak. In tears, she begged the court's forgiveness for her lies, and asked forgiveness of Ntanturo's family. She said she knew she was guilty before God, but that she had been forgiven by him. The court accepted her penitence and she was not tried for perjury.

Next day, she received from Ntanturo a letter which she still treasures. "My beloved daughter," he wrote, "I have such a deep love for you now that you have spoken the truth. As you wept in court yesterday, I realised the depth of your sorrow for what you have done. I now want to honour you as a member of my family. I want our hearts to be one. I will not be a bad parent to you, and will give you a father's gift when your next child is born. The doors of my family are always open to you whenever you come. My daughter, I want to thank you. If ever you have a problem, don't hesitate to come to me or my family for help. What you did yesterday will never be forgotten. The other prisoners here greet you. Read these Bible verses for your comfort: Numbers 6:24–26; Hebrews 13:18–19; Romans 9:25–29; Psalms 26, 25 and 35; 1 Timothy 1:1–18." He asked for photos of her family and gave her a New Testament with Psalms.

Two months later, after another hearing, he was released. He gave her a beautiful photo frame, which he had made in prison, for the pictures she had sent him. On the reverse was painted, "We praise God in Jesus Christ our Lord who has helped us to be reconciled. Romans 5:1–11." He has continued to keep in touch with Chantal and gave her a father's gift on the birth of her next child.

It was easy to make false accusations against innocent people, and hard for those so accused to forgive their accusers, yet the prisons are also packed with those who are guilty of involvement in the genocide. The prisons were full to overflowing and it was calculated that it would take about 300 years to give everyone a fair trial. The international community was criticising Rwanda for the inhuman conditions in the jails. It is a recognised maxim that "justice delayed is justice denied". The Rwandan government decided to return to the traditional forms of justice in an effort to clear the enormous backlog of cases to be heard.

In November 1994, the UN Security Commission set up the International Criminal Tribunal for Rwanda at Arusha, to try those who were guilty of organising the genocide. Those tried at Arusha could not be sentenced to death in accordance with international law and the procedures were so complicated and alien to the Rwandan way of thinking that, to most of them, Arusha was totally irrelevant. This was emphasised when one defendant who was regarded as one of the worst of the *genocidaires* was released on a technicality. Those perpetrators of the genocide who had been captured by the RPF were put on trial in Kigali, with the trials broadcast on national radio. Twenty-two of those found guilty were publicly executed in April 1998, in a cathartic act of symbolic justice, despite international outcry. Although several others have been sentenced to death, I shall be surprised if there is another such public execution.

Many Rwandans believe that to forgive someone involves ignoring the consequences of wrong actions, and that forgiveness encourages impunity. Antoine Rutayisire says that this has come about because the approach to justice brought into Rwanda by the European colonisers was retributive, whereas the traditional system of justice, *Gacaca*, was restorative.

Originally in Rwanda, no individual was ever considered to have committed an offence; it was regarded as having been committed by the whole family. In *Gacaca*, the family of the offender would sit with the family of the victim before the village elders. They would determine the truth of what happened, and establish the *icyiru* or compensation which needed to be paid to cancel the offence. Sometimes it was considered trivial enough for no *icyiru*, and they received *imbabazi* or mercy.[3] Sometimes they agreed on the number of cows to be paid in restitution as the *icyiru*, so as to re-establish a relationship between the two families. Occasionally, the offence was considered so great that no *imbabazi* could be extended, and no reconciliation was possible. These families were *inzigo* or totally incompatible, with a great gulf between them.

When a person became a Christian and felt that he ought not to live with this barrier, forgiving the offender could mean being thrown out of his own family circle as a traitor. This was what Antoine faced when he became a Christian.[4]

If a man wanted to marry a girl, the senior family member on each side would research deeply into family relationships to make sure there was no *inzigo* between them which would constitute a barrier to their marriage. Rwandans still do this, but now it is mostly ritual or play-acting. In the past it was deadly serious. If a problem developed between married couples, the elders of the family would be mediators, hearing the case and ensuring that the blame was properly apportioned. The one who accepted the blame had to confess it before the elders and swear not to repeat it. This public confession helped him not to repeat the offence.

With the coming of the Europeans, people came to be regarded as individuals who had to pay the penalty for their own offence, and this family solidarity was lost, along with the sense of the need for restitution to restore a relationship. Christianity, as taught by Europeans influenced by Greek thought, laid the stress on individual sin, individual repentance and individual forgiveness. Yet Hebrew thought forms are much closer to the African approach in their stress on family responsibility. For instance, after the battle of Jericho, Achan looted some property in direct disobedience to God's orders as relayed by Joshua. The next time they went out to fight at Ai, the Israelites were defeated. God revealed that someone had taken objects which were to have been devoted to him. By a process of elimination Achan was discovered to be the thief. Joshua told him to give glory to God by confessing what he had done. What many Europeans find hard to understand, but what is quite natural to Rwandans, is that Achan's whole family were stoned with him.[5] They were *inzigo* and could have no further place in the people of Israel.

Antoine believes that the hand of God can be seen in this return to restorative justice in the *Gacaca* courts with their emphasis on confession, restitution, forgiveness and reconciliation. AEE has been involved in training Christians throughout the country, helping them to see that it is essential to co-operate with the judicial system of the country. Throughout the land are large roadside signs about *Gacaca*. "Tell what you know. Admit what you have done. The truth will heal the land."

In *Gacaca*, the whole community is involved. Persons of good standing[6] have been elected from each Parish Council area, and have been trained in the judicial process. These are courts with the same judicial powers as any other court in the country. Four categories of crimes can be tried at different levels, with appeal at the higher level.

Category I crimes were committed by the *genocidaires*: those who planned, ordered or forced others to take part in the genocide or crimes against humanity; those in positions of authority who committed such crimes or encouraged others to do so; those who killed several people, either in their own areas or elsewhere; and rapists or those who gave women no alternative but to sleep with them for their protection. These people can only be tried by due judicial processes, not *Gacaca*. Those who are found guilty but still deny their guilt are sentenced to death or to life imprisonment. If they accept their guilt, their sentence may be reduced to 25 years.

Category II crimes were committed by those who killed, yet are not in Category I; those who beat up someone so that he died; and those who wounded someone intending death. These people are tried at the District Council level with appeal at County Council level. If they deny their guilt they may receive 25 years imprisonment or life. If they accept their guilt, this sentence can be reduced to twelve to fifteen years.

Category III is for those who did not intend death, or who were not actively involved in killing, but as a result of whose actions people died or were abused. These people are tried at Local Council level with appeal to the District Council. If they refuse to accept their guilt they receive prison terms of five to seven years; if they accept it, only three to five years.

Finally Category IV is for offences against property and livestock. They can be tried at Parish Council level. They will be assessed for compensation by the *Gacaca* who will supervise their payment.

In every case, if offenders confess before the preliminary hearings, their sentences are reduced still further. Where someone has confessed, he or she will serve half of their sentence in prison and the other half in specified community service. The confessions must be in due form to the court, and the crime described in detail. Others involved in the crime must be named, and the perpetrator must ask for the court's mercy.

The idea is for the community to be involved in trying these cases, with witnesses telling what they saw and heard. If they refuse to do so, or if they are found guilty of lying, the courts have the power to imprison them for one to three years, which was Chantal's fear.[7] In this way, it is hoped that the truth will be revealed, and perpetrators sentenced. If they are truly repentant, they will receive mercy at the hands of the community, represented by the *Gacaca* courts. Survivors will be able to have closure on their grief when they learn what happened to their loved ones.

Obviously, Hutu committed many gross human rights violations during the genocide, but such violations were also committed by the RPF, in massacres at Byumba or the Kibeho camp, for example. The *Gacaca* courts are only being used to try offenders in the genocide, and many who suffered in Byumba are saying that the *Gacaca* procedures have nothing to do with them and do not wish to attend. These offences are said to have happened as acts of war. In some cases the soldiers accused have been tried by military courts. Since they are not addressed in the same way as the genocide massacres, this has created resentment among the Hutu population. True reconciliation may be impossible in this country, until all human rights violations are seen to be punished in the same way.

Often Rwandans ask how the concept of forgiveness relates to that of justice. Does forgiveness mean that the perpetrator must escape the consequences of his crime? How do justice and mercy relate to each other? Many Rwandans consider that as Christians it would be wrong to take someone to the courts. They read what Paul says in Romans 12:17–21 and say that a Christian who has forgiven must not take any further action. These verses certainly forbid Christians to take private revenge, leaving the offender rather to God's justice, but the the next chapter[8] speaks of the role of the state in keeping order.

The government of a nation may not see its proper role as God's instrument for good. Paul wrote his letters when Nero was emperor. Nero would have laughed to think that he was in power because the Creator God had allowed it. After all, he considered himself to be divine and above the law. Yet some form of law is better than the chaos of total anarchy. Paul always admonishes the authorities when they have gone beyond their legal powers. In Philippi, for instance, he refused to leave quietly after being beaten and imprisoned illegally. Instead he expected the magistrates to apologise and escort him from the city.[9]

1 Corinthians 6:1–8 is another passage frequently quoted by those who say that it is wrong to take people to court. Here Paul is speaking to Christians who are taking their fellow believers to court in trivial lawsuits, when rather the church leaders ought to be mediating between them. This is not referring to offences committed against society, which should be tried by society.

A church teacher asked: "How can I report someone whom I have forgiven to the courts when I know it will mean a death sentence?" Hard as it may seem, it is not for an individual to make that decision. God has given that authority to the state. If the judge asks the wronged person what he or she wants to happen to the accused, as is usually the case in Rwanda, he may say, "I have forgiven them. Please exercise mercy." It is still for the court to pass sentence.

Immediately before the genocide, numbers of people were tortured and killed with apparent impunity. Reflecting on the catastrophe in the J C Jones lecture in 1995, the then General Secretary of Mid-Africa Ministry (CMS), Roger Bowen, said,

> The history of Rwanda and Burundi is scarred by outbreaks of appalling ethnic conflict of an horrific nature. In all cases there has never been a bringing to justice of the major perpetrators. A climate of impunity has been created which gives the impression that people can get away with such behaviour without fear of being brought to trial. There is little doubt that the assassination of President Ndadaye of Burundi in October 1993, and the fact that no one had been brought to justice for that event, gave the green light to the Rwandan Government that they too could get away with their genocidal plans without fear of arrest and trial. Prior to the genocide in Rwanda there had been outbreaks of ethnic violence and considerable abuse of human rights, yet the churches failed to call for the perpetrators to be brought to justice and for justice to be seen to be done. The climate of impunity created a climate of confidence for those bent on maintaining their power and influence at all costs.[10]

Monbourquette says: "Forgiveness that does not fight injustice, far from being a sign of strength and courage, shows weakness and false tolerance. It encourages the offender to repeat the crime. This is what some bishops failed to understand when they did not intervene quickly or decisively after being told about the sexual abuses committed by certain members of the clergy."[11]

The question of impunity for offenders in South Africa was one of the greatest barriers to agreement when the Truth and Reconciliation Commission was instituted. In a symposium on theological and psychological reflections on Truth and Reconciliation, Terry Dowdall speaks about impunity:

> At worst it constitutes – either *de jure* or *de facto* – a blanket absolution and protection for those who committed crimes 'in the line of duty'; and a situation where these crimes are concealed and never confirmed or condemned by the authorities of the country. It sends an unequivocal message: it's OK to torture, rape and murder people if you do it under the umbrella of any regime's policies and orders. Impunity means never having to say you're sorry, and never having to pay for your crimes. And, of course, impunity reassures the population of abusers – those still in office and those that occupy such posts in the future – that work as a torturer/killer is still a career option. To the extent that we condone it we risk perpetuating abusive patterns [...]
>
> Any political movement that argues that torture or arbitrary murder are somehow more acceptable in the service of *their* ends becomes fatally compromised, and lays the ground for future abuse. For this reason it is important that gross human rights abuses are recorded and treated in the same way regardless of whether they were perpetrated by the former regime or by the liberation movements.[12]

It was clearly established in 1946, in the judgement which followed the international trial of the Nazi leaders at Nuremberg after the genocide of the Jews, that it was no excuse to say that atrocities were committed on the orders of a senior officer. Everyone needs to take responsibility for his or her own action, although the courts may take the circumstances into account in mitigation.

AEE has done much to encourage Christians to take full part in the *Gacaca* system, seeing this as a way to set the record straight and to ensure that a climate of impunity never again prevails in Rwanda. They have also trained lay counsellors, 60 in every county, to support those on the bench of judges, many of whom are Christians. Some are also pastors who receive much abuse for mixing religion and politics.

In January 2003, realising that many of those in prison had already served a longer time than they would receive as sentence, the president decreed that some 19,000 prisoners were to be released, although they would still have to appear before the *Gacaca*. They were those who had no dossier proving a case against them, the sick, and those over 70 years old or under twelve years old when they were imprisoned. Those who had already accepted their guilt and confessed in due form were also released. Many of these people had accepted that their sin had been transferred to the cross of Jesus, through the efforts of AEE and many other Christian organisations with a prison ministry. The release of these prisoners has resulted in the reopening of wounds for many people in the community.

Initially, the released prisoners were sent to various rehabilitation camps around the country, where church members were allowed to visit them. At one such camp at Gisenyi, AEE were allowed to conduct a seminar there. When a Tutsi member of the team acknowledged that many of those in prison were innocent of the crimes of which they were accused, and confessed the sins of Tutsi in the time of the monarchy, and some of the crimes committed during and since the war, the hearts of many of the prisoners were touched, and they were able to talk about what they had done.

Several AEE seminars, following the release of prisoners, have brought together the families of the victims and those of the prisoners, in preparation for the *Gacaca* courts. Many of those in prison have no dossier supporting the allegations against them, so government officials have taken them to the areas where they were supposed to have killed in an effort to find out the truth. It was hoped that in this way, they could be released if no evidence was found against them. However, it is often found that the Tutsi in those areas are still filled with anger and accuse the prisoners, even though their evidence is inconsistent. Meanwhile many Hutu blindly support their relatives, denying their guilt, so that it is often impossible to find the truth.

In one area, Lawrence,[13] a Tutsi, could not bear the thought of any of the accused coming home, feeling that he would not be responsible for his own actions if they did. He would tell the investigators that the accused had indeed killed but that the family of the victims had moved elsewhere. In this way he had blocked the return of any of the accused in that area. In 2003, Lawrence attended one of the AEE seminars and saw his lies for what they were: sin that had been carried by Jesus on the cross. The next time the prosecutors brought prisoners to his home area, he admitted that he had previously been lying out of anger. Eleven innocent prisoners were finally released.

In the same seminar, Frederick,[14] the son of one of the prisoners, was helped. He believed that his father was innocent because he could not bear the thought that he might be a killer. He had been angry with all the Tutsi in the area, because he saw them as having accused an innocent man, despite a sneaking fear that his father might indeed be a killer. After the seminar, Frederick asked a member of the team, a pastor, to accompany him to the prison to see his father. The pastor explained to the father that the seminar had prepared the young man's heart to hear the truth, whatever it was. "Whatever you have done, your son will not condemn you," he said. "Please tell the truth now." The father let out a huge sigh of relief. "Yes," he said, "I did kill several people. I could not admit this before because of the shame I felt. I feared what it would do to my family." Frederick was shattered, but after a moment said, "I am still your son, and will continue to be so, despite this." The prisoner was very grateful to the AEE team for enabling him to speak the truth, and he fully confessed to the authorities, giving them the names of those he had killed.

"When we go to prisons to preach the gospel, or when prisoners hear the gospel on the radio, many repent and know that they are forgiven by God," said Joseph of AEE. "It is much harder for them to confess to the authorities. They feel shame, and dread to see the reactions of their friends and families. As for confessing what they have done to the families of their victims, that is truly difficult."

Richard[15] had listened to Antoine preaching in prison. Later he said, "You AEE people have been such a blessing to me. I never killed anyone and was very bitter that I had been imprisoned. I realised after your visit that I was indeed guilty. I may not have killed, but I had participated in groups that did. I had searched for Tutsi who were later killed, and I had looted their homes. I can now accept my sin. I have confessed to the authorities and now I can be released."

There is, however, a difference between confession and repentance. In the old system of *Gacaca* and even now with family disputes, the offender was expected to confess publicly what he had done: *kwatura*. This did not necessarily mean that he was sorry but the public confession ensured that others would be watching and helping him not to reoffend. Repentance, *kwihana*, implies a genuine sorrow for what happened and a determination, from within, not to repeat the offence. The Kinyarwanda word *kwihana* literally means "to punish oneself" and involves an acceptance of guilt. The biblical view of confession is to say publicly that we agree with God's view of sin (from the two Latin words *con* = with and the past participle of *fateri* = avow). The Greek word for repentance, *metanoia*, goes even further than the Kinyarwanda since it means that there is a complete change of direction. To repent involves a genuine sorrow for the offence as well as a determination to change one's lifestyle completely so that one does not even wish to reoffend. Many prisoners have confessed their crimes (*kwatura*) in the expectation of receiving mercy in the courts and a reduced sentence. All the Christian agencies working in the prisons are helping them to see the need for genuine repentance before God, and to accept his view of their condition. Only then is true forgiveness possible, and this paves the way for true reconciliation.

Notes

1. See Edward's story in chapter 1
2. Not her real name
3. The same word is used for forgiveness, which gives rise to confusion
4. See chapter 3 for his story
5. See Joshua 7 for the whole story of Achan
6. Many of these people have been through the seminars run by AEE or one of the other Christian organisations involved in healing and reconciliation
7. See Leviticus 5:1
8. Romans 13:1–7
9. Acts 16:37–39; see also Acts 22:23–29
10. Quoted in Rutayisire, 1995, p 123
11. Monbourquette, 2000, p 38
12. Botman and Petersen, 1996, p 29
13. Not his real name
14. Not his real name
15. Not his real name

CHAPTER EIGHT

Forgiveness and rape

"Our hope for you is unshaken; for we know that as you share in our sufferings, you will also share in our comfort." *(2 Corinthians 1:7, RSV)*

Rape is considered a Category I crime in the *Gacaca* courts, on the same level as multiple murder and planning the genocide, since it was used as a weapon of war in Rwanda. It will probably never be known how many women, and children as young as two, were raped in the genocide. Part of the general strategy was to humiliate Tutsi women, hoping that they would die, either as a result of gang rapes or of sadness and shame later. Indeed, many did die of their injuries and mutilations following the rape, and many are still dying as a result of AIDS contracted at that time.[1] Not only Tutsi women suffered in this way; most of the Hutu women in the Byumba area were raped by the RPF soldiers in the years before the genocide.

Based on the number of pregnancies as a result of rape (between 2,000 and 5,000), one United Nations reporter estimated that between 250,000 and 500,000 must have been raped during the war of 1990–94.[2] Accurate information is scarce, because rape is hidden. In Rwanda even a widow is regarded as "used goods" and very rarely remarries. Rape is regarded as so shameful that many have never told anyone, but continue to exist, feeling shamed and soiled, and living with the fear of AIDS. Now, ten years on, many of those women are indeed dying from the disease.

Often, women were raped by neighbours or people they

knew, which adds to their reluctance to talk, for fear of reprisals from those still living near them. Frequently, women were taken under the "protection" of one man, and forced into a pretence of marriage. These women generally feel a sense of shame at the way they survived, and indeed may be objects of scorn to others. Sometime a group of women were kept for the use of a band of militia, whose one desire was to humiliate them in every way possible, as a deliberate act of aggression against Tutsi women.

Human Rights Watch describe how rape and sexual violence was used to violate the entire community, yet say,

> In Rwanda, as elsewhere in the world, rape and other gender-based violations carry a severe social stigma. The physical and psychological injuries suffered by Rwandan rape survivors are aggravated by a sense of isolation and ostracism. Rwandan women who have been raped or suffered sexual abuse, generally do not dare reveal their experiences publicly, fearing that they will be rejected by their family and wider community and that they will never be able to reintegrate or to marry. Others fear retribution from their attacker if they speak out. Often, rape survivors suffer extreme guilt for having survived and been held for rape, rather than having been executed.[3]

Ruth[4] was born on the outskirts of Kigali, and was married in 1989. In the 1994 genocide, most of her family was killed, including her parents, husband and three-year-old child. Alone and expecting her second child, she fled towards Congo, helped by a Christian Hutu friend. He protected her as far as Gisenyi where, in the general chaos, they were separated. She continued into Congo but was captured by the *interahamwe*, and for the next few months was held captive under appalling conditions in a refugee camp near Goma.

During that time, she was repeatedly raped by so many men she could not count them. She was prevented from getting the refugee's allowance of food and clothing, and nearly starved. A local Congolese Christian, Felicien, found her half dead and nearly naked. He called some white aid workers, explaining that she was a Tutsi woman in fear of her life among all the Hutu. They took her to a doctor, and for the next two months she was cared for in hospital where she gave birth to a baby girl. The aid workers built a hut for her, and told her that they would keep an eye on her and she would be safe. However, a few days later, when she returned to her hut after collecting some food, she found it had been burnt down and her possessions destroyed.

The aid workers offered her a job looking after seven orphans outside the camp. One of her duties was to attempt to find their families, which meant returning to the camp, accompanying the aid workers. On one occasion, she was recognised by a woman who called out, "This Tutsi is like a rat, able to find a life after everything."

Eventually, Ruth heard that one aunt, married to a Hutu, was still alive in Kigali. She sought help from the United Nations Commission for Refugees to return. However, the day she went for help, the building was attacked by the *interahamwe*. Ruth ran from the fighting and fell into a hole, seriously injuring her baby. After treatment at the First Aid Centre, she was able to set out for Kigali. After some weeks on the journey, she was reunited with her aunt.

A year later, the aunt died and the husband threw her out of his home. She was helped by a government society, set up to help those who had been raped in the war. They found her a house and advised her to test for HIV/AIDS. "I was frightened and refused," she said. "I thought that if I found I had the disease, I would commit suicide."

In 2002, she married a soldier, and a year later had a baby boy. About that time she met John Gakwandi, and was introduced to Solace Ministries. He told her that anyone with difficulties was welcomed, and they helped her to tell her story, at first with a social worker but eventually in a group therapy session of both Hutu and Tutsi. "At last I have found people who will listen to me, and pray with me. I have found friends who have needs like mine which we can share. Above all I have found peace in my heart."

John persuaded her to be tested for HIV/AIDS, assuring her that she was not alone. In June 2003, she tested positively. Her husband was fighting in Congo and she did not know how to tell him. She was very grateful for the support that she received from Solace Ministries. "I know that there are many women like me in Rwanda. I can only pray, and I know that God is near. I have asked for his forgiveness, and he has helped me to forgive those who harmed me," she said. "I praise the Lord for Solace Ministries. They are a group of people who listen and yet do not blame. Their Bible teaching has helped so much. They have comforted me in my pain. I'm now able to be with other Hutu. I know they are not all to blame for what some of them did. They were not all bad. I'm now praying that I will be healed."

Solace Ministries spend much of their time with raped women, listening to their stories as they can bear to tell them, praying with them and, above all, accepting them. Many experienced repeated rapes, and were often left naked by the side of the road with their legs outspread, as objects of contempt, discarded things. Often they crawled, naked and bleeding, until they found a compassionate person to take them in. Shame and lack of funds prevented them from seeking medical help, and many still suffer from injuries received. Their shame gives them a sense of isolation, and the way the Solace team members accept them plays a valuable role in their healing. Thinking about Jesus hanging naked on the cross, the cynosure of all who passed by, brings great empathy. Most pictures of the crucifixion have Jesus decently covered with a loin cloth, and many find it hard to believe that he was naked.

What a comfort to know that he does understand their shame, and carried it for them so that they no longer need to bear it.

Since the war, rape is increasingly common. One reason is a myth, which must be demonic in origin and which many believe, that to sleep with a virgin will cure AIDS. Another reason is that men who are not themselves infected believe that only virgins can provide safe sex. Consequently, many younger and younger women, even children, are raped. Christian leaders need urgent teaching about how to help these damaged women in their congregations.

The founder and Director of Solace Ministries, John Gakwandi,[5] had been an *Assistant Médical* running a Health Clinic for the National Bank of Rwanda before the war. He and his family were miraculously protected during the genocide but were in hiding for 89 days. When it was over, John found that he had lost 99 members of his family on his father's side alone. During that horrific time he felt convinced that God was calling him to a new ministry, and said, "If I survive this I will serve you with my whole life, particularly helping widows and orphans."

After the war, he took a job at the local hospital, but within a week knew that this was no longer for him. The organisation Compassion asked him to oversee their orphanage work. The thought excited him, but as he prayed he became less comfortable with the idea. After that, World Relief gave him a job as part of their widows' work. At first, they had meetings for the local church leaders to ask the hard questions: How can we rebuild the credibility of the church? Where do we start? How can we help the widows and orphans? How can this country see reconciliation?

John found that he was assigned to give out material aid to the many widows who came in great need. As he spoke to them, he realised that often their pain was too deep for words. He would spend time sitting with them, and gradually they opened up, telling horrific stories of suffering. "They had been so helped by having someone to talk to," he said, "that often they would leave without the material objects they had come for. Often they would cry, and the tears brought some measure of healing."

John started crying out to God, "Lord, what should we do to help these women? Their pain is so great. How do we begin?" He heard the Lord answer, "Comfort my people." As he read his Bible, it was as if every word shouted out, "Comfort!" Two verses in particular stood out. "Comfort, yes, comfort my people, says your God",[6] and God "comforts us in all our tribulation, that we may be able to comfort those who are in any trouble, with the comfort with which we ourselves are comforted by God".[7]

John said, "I started asking, 'How do I comfort?' If someone lost a prized possession like a watch one might be able to comfort by buying a replacement, but we cannot bring back the dead. A person is unique. Even though a widow might remarry, she still feels the loss of her first husband. She might have other children, but nothing can replace the child she has lost. I realised that though I had lost my father, mother, brothers, friends, my home and most of my possessions, yet I had peace in my heart. I began to ask myself, 'Where does this peace come from?' I realised that it was Jesus. Knowing Jesus, and having him in my heart, is what gives me peace. I thought that the main way that I could comfort others with the comfort I had received, was to help them to find Jesus for themselves."

In December 1995, he started holding meetings for widows in the World Relief buildings. Only eight came to the first meeting, but soon 140 widows were meeting regularly. He shared his vision with a few friends and his colleagues, and in June 1996 he started Solace Ministries, still operating from the World Relief buildings. In October 2000, they were able to move to their own premises.

From the first, John realised that they would need to help

some people in material ways as well as praying with and for them. He could help through World Relief, but if he wanted to start his own ministry, where would the money come from? "I realised that everything that I had received had come from God and was his. If I wanted to be used by him, I needed to put everything I possessed at his disposal to use as he wanted. I committed myself first of all, and then all my resources, to these widows through God. Those who join us in the Ministry are expected to do the same. It is a full commitment. We have received other funds from other sources who have given us grants, but the first funding comes from ourselves, and God has blessed us in it."

Solace has moved to purpose-built premises, where there is a meeting room and small counselling rooms as well as offices. It has already outgrown the original building, and a large Conference Centre is being built to accommodate the more than 500 widows who meet together some weeks. The main focus of their ministry is to allow hurting people to talk. Initially, this takes place in individual counselling sessions, but later they may go into group therapy, where hearing stories from the other ethnic group frequently brings healing.

"There is such a wall between Hutu and Tutsi in this country," says John, "but as you break down the wall, and bring people together to hear each other's stories, they begin to lose their attitudes of judgement against the other group, and the Lord breaks down the barriers. They begin to trust each other."

In Solace, people whose families have been destroyed find a family to support and help them. Many who come are consumed with feelings of anger and hatred, or feel totally rejected by society. John says that talking to such people about forgiveness only brings further feelings of guilt and rejection by God. As they find acceptance within the Solace family, with no attitude of condemnation whatever crimes they admit, many find that they can love again. They are able to receive talk about forgiveness, and many have been able to forgive from their heart, as they find forgiveness in Jesus.

Hardest is to learn to forgive themselves. Many of the women who come to Solace feel guilty because they have survived when thousands did not. They are filled with anguish that they were unable to help their loved ones who were killed or at least to die with them. Often they feel guilty because their survival resulted from being used by the soldiers or *interahamwe* and they feel contaminated and dirty as a result. One woman said that she always felt naked and exposed. As they are healed from their inner pain, the women find that they are able to face the reality of what happened and to forgive themselves, even to realise that they were not guilty of anything more than survival. Many have found that the healing of inner pain has brought healing from physical sickness.

Solace Ministries seek to help at every level. They help the needy with school fees or materials for schoolchildren; they engage lawyers for those who need them; they join together to build houses or repair damaged ones; they support child-headed families, handicapped people or those living with AIDS. A large section of their work is in helping women who were sexually abused in the war, or since, many of whom have found out that they are now living with HIV/AIDS. Solace provides teaching on care and prevention of HIV/AIDS. They also hold seminars on Christian Counselling, Business Management and Prison Ministry. "We are not competing with other ministries," says John. "We are complementary to each other. The need is so vast that I wish dozens of other Christian ministries existed to meet it."

As part of their regular ministries, they have meetings on Sunday, twice a month, and every second Wednesday when any who have been helped by Solace can pray for each other and the nation and praise God for what he is doing amongst them. They can introduce friends to the Solace Ministry at these meetings. Twice a month, on Saturday, a meeting is held to support those who have been raped or are suffering from HIV/AIDS. Barriers are broken down when they study the Bible together or work together on a project such as building a house for a fellow-member in need.

All that they do has the purpose of helping traumatised people find the love and comfort of Jesus Christ as their Redeemer. Anybody hurting is welcome, regardless of ethnicity, and their main aim is to bring reconciliation to the land.

AEE deal with the subject of rape in a follow-up session for Christian leaders. They are told that ideally, it should be a woman who counsels a rape victim, as she may find it very hard to trust another man. If possible, each church should train a group of women who can help them. Church leaders should address the subject of rape in a general way in sermons, making it clear that they understand something of the trauma these women endured, and that they want to help those who are still carrying this secret.

Many Christians in Rwanda see rape as a sin that needs to be confessed by the victim, and they have to be taught that these women have been sinned against, and are as much victims as those who were mutilated with limbs cut off in the genocide.

Raped women feel:[8]

- devalued and worthless. If they were virgins it is unlikely that they will ever marry, and many become prostitutes;
- dirty and contaminated;
- guilty, even though it was not their fault;
- a deep sense of shame;
- angry and unable to relate to men;
- wounded at the very core of their being and filled with pain, which is frequently suppressed because they do not feel safe enough to acknowledge what happened to anyone;
- fearful that they might be pregnant, or have contracted a disease, particularly AIDS, which can take several years to manifest itself. All women are encouraged to test for

HIV/AIDS and now, ten years after the war, many find their fears were justified.

In the AEE seminars, they discuss John 10:10 (NIV). "'The thief comes only to kill, steal and destroy'. Satan has robbed raped women of many things: peace, joy, purity, innocence, virginity, value, dignity, the right to make good decisions about their own bodies, hope for a happy marriage, health, etc. But John 10:10 goes on to say, 'I have come that they may have life, and have it to the full.' Praise God that Jesus has come to restore all that the thief has stolen from us!"[9]

Some of the verses which have been found helpful, which tell of God's desire to restore us, include:

"For I will restore health to you and heal you of your wounds," says the Lord, "because they called you an outcast..." (Jeremiah 30:17)

So I will restore to you the years that the swarming locust has eaten... (Joel 2:25)

He restores my soul... (Psalm 23:3)

You, who have shown me great and severe troubles, shall revive me again, and bring me up again from the depths of the earth. You shall increase my greatness, and comfort me on every side. (Psalm 71:20–21)

And after you have suffered a little while, the God of all grace, who has called you to his eternal glory in Christ, will himself restore, establish and strengthen you. (1 Peter 5:10, RSV)

"I have seen his ways, and will heal him; I will also lead him, and restore comforts to him and to his mourners. I create the fruit of the lips: Peace, peace to him who is far off and to him who is near," says the Lord, "and I will heal him." (Isaiah 57:18–19)

Kinyarwanda has no gender-specific pronouns, so that this last verse would be more helpful to a rape victim there who can find it referring to her, than perhaps it would be in the English-speaking world, where she might feel it is referring to her violator! In the AEE seminars, when a rape victim has the courage to admit what happened to her, the confession of men on the team, standing in the gap has helped the victim to forgive.

When praying for a rape victim, the team members have found that it is helpful to pray in the following ways:[10]

1 Rather than speaking about the cleansing blood of Jesus they have found it more helpful to pray for cleansing in the living water of God's Holy Spirit, not to remove their own sin, since they were not guilty of the rape, but to remove the contaminating sin of the man or men who violated them, cleansing their bodies, minds, emotions and spirits from all that makes them feel dirty. "Then I will sprinkle clean water on you and you shall be clean; I will cleanse you from all your filthiness ... "[11]

2 For the women to be released from any false guilt that they may have been carrying, again stressing that they had been unable to prevent the rape. However, it may be appropriate for them to seek forgiveness for their sinful response to the rape such as anger or hatred.

3 For them to be released from their shame. Jesus suffered shame on the cross so that we might receive his glory.

Some verses which help are:[12]

It is for your sake that I have borne reproach, that shame has covered my face [...] You know the insults I receive, and my

shame and dishonour; my foes are all known to you. Insults
have broken my heart, so that I am in despair; I looked for pity
but there was none; and for comforters, but I found none.
(Psalm 69:7, 19–20, NRSV)

Look to him, and be radiant; so your faces shall never be
ashamed. (Psalm 34:5, NRSV)

My people shall never again be put to shame. (Joel 2:27b,
NRSV)

Since you were precious in my sight, you have been honoured,
and I have loved you ... Everyone who is called by my name,
whom I have created for my glory ... [13] (Isaiah 43:4a, 7a)

Tori Dante, in her honest book describing ongoing sexual
abuse from her father that she suffered from the age of four,
was particularly helped by Psalm 27:10, "When my father and
mother forsake me, then the Lord will take care of me." At the
time she felt rejected by both parents, since her mother had
sided with her father during the court case.[14] In situations of
child abuse like this, often the mother simply cannot handle
hearing accusations against her husband, and apparently
rejects her daughter in self-defence.

Unlike those who experienced rape during the war in
Rwanda, Tori's situation involved long-held and deep-seated
pain, which she had disguised in a conspiracy of silence. Only
when she became a Christian did the Lord help her to face her
pain. After her father was imprisoned, she found that first she
had to deal with her anger. Gradually, as the rage diminished,
she was able to face more of her pain. Often she screamed at
God, asking him to deal with it, once and for all, but he did not.

I've since had it explained to me that because my experience
of sexual abuse started at a young age, as most abuse cases do,

and because I was abused frequently and for a long time, my identity had got caught up with it. I was not the person I could have been if I had had different parents. My entire experience consisted of being a girl who had to stay quiet and keep dark secrets. I was a girl who was emotionally damaged, who felt nobody could be trusted and nobody could help. I knew in my head that God could help me, but at first I was scared of the pain I might have to go through. If God had taken all the garbage away in one operation, I would have been left with a gaping hole. Yes, God could fill that, but the shock would have been traumatic and I had already been through enough traumas. I would have panicked if it had all gone at once. Who would I be? If there was no pain involved, what would I learn? What would I do with the new me? There would have been a sense of loss, which sounds strange. But the pain I had was familiar and made me feel secure, which is hard to for me admit now.[15]

Many children in Rwanda would identify with Tori, not through sexual but physical abuse from drunken fathers. Like her, they find the idea of the Fatherhood of God hard to reconcile with their experience of abusive fathers. Both Joseph and Anastase needed healing from the wounds of childhood, and have been enabled to forgive abusive fathers, through AEE seminars. Now they stand in the gap as fathers whenever anyone reveals the pain of an abused childhood. Although many people have been healed of their pain at one seminar, and been enabled to forgive, many others, like Odette,[16] have needed several seminars before they can face their pain. It is important not to pre-empt the Holy Spirit's timing, or to force something the people are not ready to address, as Tori came to understand.

In the AEE seminars, having prayed for raped women, specifically praying for their negative view of themselves to be taken away, the team members pray for restoration of all that Satan had stolen from them. "It is important to name all the things God wants to restore to them (see the list above of what Satan has robbed them of) and pray specifically for each aspect to be restored. They need to know that we also value, respect and honour them. It is good to end by affirming them and building up their self-esteem."[17] They then affirm the women's value in God's eyes using various verses from the Bible which speak of the delight he takes in his people.[18]

Finally, they take on the priestly role and pronounce a blessing over the wounded person, specifically blessing her sexuality that it might be sanctified once more, and over her life using blessings such as those found in Numbers 6:24–26; Psalm 115:15; 129:8b; 134:3; Hebrews 13:20–21; Jude 24–25.[19]

Children conceived as a result of rape are often rejected by the mother, though Rwandans love children and others may take them in. They may grow up feeling unwanted and rejected, believing that their birth was a terrible mistake, and that he or she should not be alive. One woman, who was raped by a soldier and who is now sick with AIDS, said in the presence of her nine-year-old daughter, "And he left me with *that*." Such a child needs much love if she is not to grow up damaged and incapable of love.

One Christian who conceived as a result of rape in the war, deliberately called her child Tumukunde which means "We love him". Her child was loved and accepted by the family. Another woman, a virgin, raped on the bodies of her relations who had just been killed, loves her child but dare not tell him of the circumstances of his conception. She has told him that his father was killed in the war. Living this lie is destroying her but she dared not do differently. Church leaders need to take the lead in showing God's love and acceptance to such women and their children, assuring them of their value in God's eyes.

It is not enough to speak about their value in God's eyes. Our attitude must prove it. Solace Ministries shows the love they need, as Ruth found. They love the women in practical ways as well as being there for them, when and if they want to talk about their experiences. Their pain may be expressed in anger against God or in suicidal depression. John Gakwandi says, "It is important not to show shock at anything we are told, but to continue to accept them whatever they say."

The most important ministry, Solace have found, is to listen. Tori Dante has this advice for Christians wanting to help victims of abuse:

- The most important factor while listening to abused people is to give them space and time and to believe them.
- Most abused people think they will not be believed. Helpers should emphasise the fact that they are there to listen, and that even though it may shock them or be painful, they will still respect and love the person. Most abused people do not disclose graphic details straight away, they usually test the water to see if and how you will respond.
- Time is important too. I know that some people want to go home after church, but if you are going to tackle this issue you must be prepared that, for people who want to talk, it may take time. It is no good telling them that they were brave for coming forward and then saying that you only have ten minutes. I know that when I first started telling people what had happened to me, all I wanted was for them to listen. I certainly did not want any advice and I certainly didn't want to hear that I had to forgive.
- Do not ask questions or lead the conversation, because questions can be attacking and make the person feel they have to take responsibility or blame someone else.
- Forgiveness shouldn't be the first thing that they are told to do; letting go is more appropriate, and is one of the translations of the Greek word that Jesus used for forgiveness.[20]

Notes

1. A harrowing account of the sufferings of women in 1994 can be found in the Human Rights Watch/Africa Book, *Shattered Lives: Sexual Violence during the Rwandan Genocide and its Aftermath*
2. Human Rights Watch, 1996, p 24
3. Ibid, p 2
4. Not her real name
5. His story is told in *Rwanda: The Land God Forgot?* (pp 230–2)
6. Isaiah 40:1
7. 2 Corinthians 1:4
8. List adapted from Lloyd with Bresser, 2001, p 103
9. Ibid
10. Ibid, with comments by the author
11. Ezekiel 36:25
12. List adapted from Lloyd with Bresser, 2001, p 103
13. See also Isaiah 54:4–5 and 61:7
14. Dante, 2001, p 129. Reproduced with permission of Hodder & Stoughton
15. Ibid, p 172
16. Her story is told in chapter 5
17. Lloyd with Bresser, 2001, p 103
18. Verses which speak of the value of God's people in his eyes: Deuteronomy 7:6–7; 14:2; 32:10; Psalm 17:8; 35:27; 36:7; 37:23–24; 107:8; 116:15; 147:11; 149:4; Proverbs 8:30–31; Isaiah 43:4; 54:10; 62:2–4; Jeremiah 31:3; 32:40–41; Lamentations 3:22–26; Hosea 11:3–4, 8; Zephaniah 3:17; Malachi 3:17; Luke 11:13; 12:32; John 3:16; Romans 8:38–39; 10:12; 2 Corinthians 8:9; Ephesians 1:7–8; 3:12–19; 5:25–27; 1 John 3:1
19. Lloyd with Bresser, 2001, p 104
20. Dante, 2001, pp 203–4. Reproduced with permission of Hodder & Stoughton

CHAPTER NINE

Forgiveness and anger

"Be angry but do not sin; do not let the sun go down on your anger and give no opportunity to the devil."
(Ephesians 4:26–27, RSV)

Many **rape victims** and widows are struggling with overwhelming anger. How do they deal with this rage? Are there ways of resolving conflict without resorting to violence? What can be learned from the events of 1994 which will help ensure that it never happens again?

The Peace-making, Healing and Reconciliation Programme (PHARP) is one of many Christian organisations involved in reconciliation in Rwanda; their main focus is on conflict resolution. When the genocide started in 1994, many Rwandan Christians studying in Nairobi found themselves swamped by the refugees pouring into Kenya. A Kinyarwanda service had been started every Sunday afternoon at the Church of the Good Shepherd by Tutsi refugees from 1959. They now opened their buildings to a new wave of Tutsi refugees. When the refugees became largely Hutu in increasing numbers, the Nazarene church followed their example. Soon the two churches had separate ethnic congregations, which brought increasing suspicion between the two communities.

Pastor Celestin Musekura was working with MAP International (Medical Assistance Programme), a Christian organisation dedicated to helping those in medical need. He had a burden for the traumatised people he was seeing daily at these churches, and started a programme of seminars, teach-

ing from the Bible on repentance, forgiveness, conflict resolution and reconciliation. In 1995, he started a programme of
teaching Christian counsellors so that they could help those
who found it impossible either to repent or to forgive. Soon
they were asked to give these seminars in the refugee camps
of Tanzania and Congo as well as amongst refugees from
Burundi who speak a very similar language and whose conflict
is on similar ethnic lines.

When, at the end of 1996, most of the refugees returned to
Rwanda, those who remained were viewed with suspicion by
the Kenyan government, who considered that they must be
interahamwe. Many, however, were simply too traumatised to
return.

A sub-section of MAP International developed called PRM
(Peace-building and Reconciliation Ministry) with several
Rwandan workers involved, and Rev Felicien Nemeyimana as
Director. They recognised the needs of traumatised people to
talk about their pain in a non-condemnatory atmosphere.
Soon they incorporated a programme for helping those with
HIV/AIDS, both in caring for those suffering from it and in
prevention of the disease.

In May 1998, Felicien found Mrs Julienne Kayijuka, whose
husband at that time was General Secretary of Scripture Union
in Rwanda; they asked her and another pastor to head up the
work of the PRM programme for MAP International in
Rwanda. He said, "We have very little money but we believe
that this is a needed programme in Rwanda at this time."

They were given a small office at the SU Headquarters and
started work, teaching in seminars throughout the country
amongst pastors and church leaders, women, and young
people. Each programme is headed by a different worker. The
subjects they taught include such subjects as: Help for
traumatised people; Peace-building and conflict resolution;
Justice; Righteousness and holy living; Reconciliation; Care
for AIDS victims and prevention of HIV/AIDS. Before a sem-

inar in any part of the country, they write to all the organisations in the area dealing with the particular people concerned, whether Christian or not, to invite them to join in the seminar.

In October 2001, MAP International, who had provided the finance and supported PRM in these ventures, felt that it was time that they withdrew and returned to their original vision of medical work. They told the PRM programme to continue with the vision that God had given them of healing and reconciliation but that they ought to find a new name; they came up with PHARP International. PHARP works in Tanzania, Kenya, Rwanda and Congo and has a vision of working in Burundi and Sudan, hoping to start an office in each country of the Great Lakes Region.

In 2003, they started a fifteen-minute radio programme once a week on Radio Rwanda and this has attracted many people to come to their seminars. It is listened to throughout the country, especially in prisons; refugees outside the country have been encouraged to return, because of what they heard on the radio.

A widow, who had already been helped by PHARP seminars, was helped by one of these radio programmes. She said, "I have lost most of my relations from one side of my family, but have many who committed atrocities on the other side. I was standing in the middle after the war. Some of my relations were killed, others are in prison, and still more are in refugee camps. I did not know what to do." PHARP training seminars helped her to see that she could stand in the gap, bringing reconciliation to both sides of the ethnic divide, and that God could create a new Rwanda of united people. Listening to a radio programme giving testimonies of those who had forgiven their husband's killers gave her joy and encouraged her as she continued her work of bringing together survivors from both groups.

Rwandan culture suppresses emotions. One pastor had never understood those who expressed strong reactions to anything. He thought of them as demonised. Listening to a radio broadcast helped him to understand the devastating reactions of traumatised people and to be more understanding in his approach to them. He went on a PHARP seminar to learn how to care for them better.

In a country like Rwanda, with such a history of conflict, anger is very common. Yet because Rwandans believe that to show anger is to give others an advantage, and because the teaching of the church has been that anger is always sinful, it is often denied or suppressed, rather than brought to the cross. Christian leaders must be taught how to handle people in their congregations who are angry, and also how to deal with their own anger.

Anger is often sparked by reminders of traumatic events, as Mary[1] found. In 1994, she had hidden in a hut behind her home where most of her family were killed. She had escaped with her little brother to the nearby church, but he was killed there. Two younger sisters survived the fighting, but her house had been burnt down and her fields taken, and she had no idea how to care for them. Having nowhere else to go, she returned to the family plot, where she rebuilt her home among neighbours who had killed her family or stood by without helping. She wanted nothing to do with them. In her loneliness, she prayed one day: "Lord, help me to be able to be with others", and felt an easing of her heart. One of her neighbours, who had tried to kill her and had killed several of her friends, became ill and died, as did his wife. "Although he had tried to kill me," she said, "I felt I could not put my hatred of him on his children, and I was helped by the Spirit to help them, and even eventually to love them."

Her younger sister had been with her mother when a grenade was thrown at them. Her mother was killed, and her sister lost a finger. "Every time I saw her hand, I became angry again. It was only the Holy Spirit who has enabled me to forgive," she said.

Anger, like fear, is in itself neutral, but can be used rightly or destructively. Learning this is often a revelation to Christians in Rwanda, and helps them to acknowledge their anger. Anger can be divided into three categories:

1 Innocent anger

This is the anger experienced by a baby who is neglected or abused before it is old enough to express it. Such anger can go deep into the soul and colour a person's attitudes to life. Often the Holy Spirit will expose this anger, and enable it to be healed.

Innocent anger is often felt in bereavement. This is not anger against anyone in particular, but at the fact of death which has separated us from our loved ones.

2 Righteous anger

This is the anger that God himself feels when he sees sin and injustice; and it is the anger we ought to feel, as well, in the face of injustice. It motivates us to do something about the situation – or it should. Nehemiah experienced this sort of anger when he heard how the nobles were exploiting the poor people in Jerusalem.[2]

Numerous examples of God's anger can be found in the Old Testament, most notably against those who constantly refused to trust him on the journey from Egypt to Canaan. Despite the miraculous way he had rescued them and provided for them in the wilderness,[3] they served other gods.[4] Later, his anger is particularly expressed against his people who practice injustice against the poor and needy.[5]

While the crucifixion of Jesus has averted God's anger from those who accept that Jesus absorbed God's anger on the cross and who are now living their lives according to his will, the New Testament has much to teach about the anger of God against those who deliberately suppress the truth and live as they please.[6] In Hebrews we are warned, "It is a fearful thing to fall into the hands of the living God",[7] and several times in the Gospels we hear that Jesus was angry:

- In Mark 3:1–5 he was angry with the Pharisees who had no compassion for the man with a withered hand, but only wanted an excuse to accuse Jesus;
- In Mark 10:13–16 he was angry with the disciples who were preventing the children from coming to him;
- In Luke 11:39–52 and again in 13:15–16 Jesus expresses his anger at the leaders of the Jews for their hypocrisy, and the way they are putting additional burdens on the people;
- In John 2:13–17 Jesus was incensed that the Jews had made the outer court of the Temple, the only area allowed to the Gentiles, into a market-place. He even made whips of cords to drive out the money changers and traders, because he was consumed with zeal for the house of the Lord.[8]

Other examples of righteous anger in the New Testament are seen when Peter confronts Ananias and Sapphira about their lies[9] and Simon the Magus about his motives in wanting the power of the Holy Spirit,[10] and when Paul confronts Elymas who tried to prevent the proconsul from believing.[11] In each of these cases, the result of their anger was to bring people to faith.[12]

The Bible tells us that God is slow to anger. He gives people every opportunity to turn back to him. He waited 400 years before bringing judgement on the tribes in Canaan with all their sexual immorality bound up in their worship of false gods, using the people of Israel as his instrument of judgement.[13] He waited over 200 years from the time Israel split away from Judah and built the two golden calves in Dan and Bethel before he brought judgement in the form of the Assyrians. He waited another 150 years before judging Judah;

and he is still waiting, wanting to give everyone the chance to repent before he brings the final judgement on the earth.[14]

God's anger is short-lived but his mercy is for ever.[15] This was a great comfort to the prophets who foresaw the judgement but knew that there would always be a remnant to declare the mercies of the Lord.[16]

3 Unrighteous anger

Because we are sinful human beings, our righteous anger is frequently, indeed usually, bound up with our own sinful reactions, so that righteous and unrighteous anger can be confused. Even innocent anger, if held onto and cherished, becomes unrighteous. Righteous anger can become unrighteous if it is expressed in an unhelpful way, thus breaking relationships, or alternatively if it is internalised, when it can lead to depression. In both instances, the good energy of anger, intended to be constructive and to right a wrong, is wasted and used destructively.

We need to learn how to deal with anger according to biblical principles. Two passages are particularly helpful:

> "Be angry and do not sin. Meditate within your heart on your bed, and be still. Offer the sacrifices of righteousness, and put your trust in the Lord." The RSV says, "Offer right sacrifices ... " (Psalm 4:4–5)

> "Be angry and do not sin; do not let the sun go down on your wrath nor give place to the devil." The NIV says, "In your anger do not sin ... " (Ephesians 4:26–27)

Both of these verses imply that it is possible to be angry without sinning. The following principles, from these passages, help us deal with our anger:

1 Do not speak out in anger, but rather take time to think about what to say, if necessary going away from the source of the anger to meditate and pray alone, "on your bed". The old advice about counting to ten before you speak is still good.

2 "Offer right sacrifices ... " The sacrificial system included the burnt offering as a sign of consecration to God, the sin offering as a sign of repentance, and the peace offering to bring reconciliation with our neighbours. In our anger we need to face what is unrighteous and to ask for God's forgiveness, as well as perhaps putting right with others what our anger might have damaged.

3 "Put your trust in the Lord", asking for his help in using righteous anger in ways that are productive, being motivated to change the situation, and trusting his mercy and forgiveness for any sinful reactions.

4 "Do not let the sun go down on your wrath ... " Holding on to anger is destructive, leading to bitterness, and sometimes destroying the body in illness.

5 "Give no place to the devil." Innocent anger in a badly abused child can open the way for demon possession. So can unrestrained anger in an adult.

Other principles which can be found in the Bible:

- Proverbs 15:1 "A soft answer turns away wrath." This is not always applicable if the other person is determined to find fault, or aggravated by a submissive attitude.
- Romans 12:19 "Beloved, do not avenge yourselves, but rather give place to wrath for it is written, 'Vengeance is mine, I will repay,' says the Lord." Biblical principles always mean that we leave vengeance to the Lord. We can never be satisfied by revenge. "If you keep on biting and devouring each other, watch out or you will be destroyed by each other." (Galatians 5:15, NIV)

- 1 Timothy 2:8 tells us that our prayers should be without anger. Angry prayers may not be not heard by God. Jesus tells us to love our enemies, to bless those who curse us and to pray for those who abuse us.[17]
- James 1:19–20 "So then, my beloved brethren, let every man be swift to hear, slow to speak, slow to wrath; for the wrath of man does not produce the righteousness of God."

"Listening to other people's anger means that we must be like sponges," says Joseph of AEE, "absorbing their pain without answering back." This does much to draw out the sting of anger. Listening is the first step in helping someone to face it and deal with it.

Anger denied and ignored can lead to much more evil, as the history of Rwanda shows. In that culture, anger should never be shown, and without permission to face the hurt and pain, it built up. In the past, a system of conflict resolution at the village elder level was restorative. This was superseded by the Belgian retributive legal system, which took justice out of the hands of the local elders and may have contributed to the build-up of anger within those who had no way of resolving it. This accumulation of anger eventually exploded in the genocide. The *Gacaca* courts are an attempt to return to the pre-European way of conflict resolution.[18]

Often something unexpected can trigger anger, or a reminder of events, as Mary found. Every time she looked at her sister's hand with its missing finger, her anger was sparked anew. A doctor was often angry at the end of a long day. She would ask the Holy Spirit to show her the cause, and as she prayed over the events of the day, she would call to mind some incident which had triggered memories of anger from the past. Facing this, she was able to deal with it before going to bed.

Monbourquette distinguishes between anger faced in a healthy way, and resentment. "Resentment is a form of disguised anger that festers around a badly healed wound."[19] Elsewhere he says, "Some people who have been hurt refuse to abandon their resentment. They fear that they will betray themselves if they let their resentment and their hatred be transformed. They believe, wrongly, that keeping their resentment alive will preserve their human dignity and keep them from risking further humiliation."[20]

He also talks about the dangers of repressed anger. "Sometimes people turn repressed anger against themselves. This happens with people who can't allow themselves even the slightest hint of anger, and feel guilty as soon as they detect such feelings in themselves. Then they blame themselves, punish themselves, or fall into a deep depression."[21]

Marie Goretti had repressed her anger against her father, but it showed in other ways. Like Chantal, she lived near the airport in Kigali. Her father's father, a Tutsi chief, had fled as a refugee in 1959; but his mother had stayed with one of her father-in-law's servants, a Hutu, eventually marrying him. Although Marie Goretti's father was Tutsi, and looked it, he was brought up by his Hutu stepfather and managed to obtain Hutu identity papers. When in turn he married, he chose a Hutu bride. He spent his life denying that he was Tutsi.

The morning after the president's plane was shot down, Marie Goretti watched a Tutsi neighbour escorted back from his place of work by a soldier. Then she heard a series of shots. On three more occasions that morning, she heard shots. Her father took to his bed out of fear that he, too, would be killed. Some of the soldiers came to the house and ordered her father to the barrier nearby, where he was taunted for his Tutsi looks, but accepted as one of them.

Meanwhile Marie Goretti's mother had heard that some friends had been killed. She went in search of them, and came back with the children whom she hid in the house. She accepted other friends, and eventually four adults and eight terrified children were hidden around the house. The *interahamwe* had heard that Tutsi were hiding there and came to search. One held Marie Goretti and said, "You are a Christian. Tell me the truth. Are there any Tutsi hidden here?" She gulped and whispered, "Yes." He looked at her for a few moments, then shouted at the others, "Get out. I have searched here and found no Tutsi."

On another occasion her father, at the barrier, heard that they were going to bring in some Hutu from a different area to kill his family by burning down the house since none of their neighbours would do so. Terrified, he rushed home to warn them. To his dismay he found Marie Goretti with some Tutsi children emerging from the toilet. He was furious. "Are there truly Tutsi hidden in our house?" he demanded. "How dare you? Do you want us to be killed for the sake of a few children?" In anger and fear, he rushed at her, raising the *muhoro* he had been given for his stint at the barrier. Seeing that he was beyond reason, Goretti said, "Get it over with quickly." Her mother, hearing the commotion, rushed out and grabbed the *muhoro*, cutting her hand as she struggled to take it from her husband. "It wasn't Goretti," she said. "It was me. I saved those children." Once he had calmed down, he asked Marie Goretti's forgiveness. He said, "Whatever happens let's die together." He went back to the barrier to tell them that he had got rid of all the Tutsi in his home.

A little later, at a different barrier where he was not known, he was beaten because they did not believe his ID card. He managed to return home, severely injured. Then the RPF captured the area, and the Hutu, including Goretti and her family, fled in fear. At a displaced persons camp in Byumba, her father went to a doctor who told him that both kidneys had been damaged in the beating, and he died shortly after they had returned home, once the fighting was over. They buried him in the environs of their house, but, deep down, Marie Goretti had never forgiven him for his attack on her, and could not mourn his death.

After the war, they heard that the two men whom they had protected had been killed elsewhere, but their widows and all the children survived, and they are still friends. Although they settled back into their home, Goretti's experiences had scarred her. A man wanted to marry her and she was interested in him, but when it came to the point, she could not. "I thought he might become like my father and kill me under pressure," she said.

She began to distrust all men. One day, her closest friend, a Hutu girl, came to see her. When she left, she said that she was going to look at her old home. It had been taken over by Tutsi soldiers who killed her. Later, when her friend's body was found, the girl's father accused Goretti of murder. Thankfully, her friend had visited someone else on the way to her home. Not finding anyone at home, she had slipped a note under the door saying where she was going. That note saved Goretti, but the experience left her in a state of shock, unable to stop weeping for her friend. "I began to hate Rwandan men," she said. "I was angry with God and asked him, 'Why did you allow me to be born a Rwandan?' About a year later I had a serious car accident, and had two weeks in hospital. I saw how the Lord still loved me by protecting me in the accident, and vowed to work for him."

In October 1996, she was working at the Trade Union Centre as a publicity officer when she met Julienne Kayijuka. Julienne was looking for someone to translate PHARP materials from English into Kinyarwanda. She started working part-time for PHARP and went to several of their seminars. At one in 1997, she met Violette, a counsellor from Nairobi. Something she said helped Goretti. "A Christian is like a rose. When you crush a rose, what comes out is a sweet smell." "Am I like a crushed rose?" she asked herself. "Is my hatred and suspicion of Rwandan men a sweet smell?"

In the same seminar, another speaker referred to John 10:10. "The thief does not come except to steal, and to kill, and to destroy. I have come that they may have life, and that they may have it more abundantly." She said, "Satan, the thief, wants to take away from us all that is good. He robs us of joy and peace and hope, so that the future no longer exists; there is no tomorrow." Goretti realised that this exactly described her state of mind. "I wanted that full life," she said, "and I started out on the road to forgiveness. It wasn't easy. Often I felt that I took one step forward, but my pain would hit again and I went back several paces."

She was by this time studying law at the university every afternoon, earning her keep three nights as a receptionist at the hospital, and three mornings working for PHARP. In November 2001 she passed her diploma in law and found a job with the justice and peace department of Trocaire, an Irish NGO, but she wanted to work full-time in peace-building and reconciliation. In February 2003, she became the communications officer for MOUCECORE, teaching in some of their seminars.

In July 2003 a PHARP speaker was talking about the way Joseph had forgiven his brothers.[22] "Have I forgiven like that?" she asked. She found that at last she was able to forgive her father. "I began to love him again," she said. "I wanted to honour his memory and so planted flowers on his grave. I also wanted to fulfil the ministry that God has given me and to be an ambassador for Christ, telling others of the reconciliation we have in him. Three passages have become very important to me: John 10:10; 2 Corinthians 5:17–21 and Ephesians 2:14."

Goretti's deep-seated anger showed in her distrust of the man who wanted to marry her, and it grew with the death of her friend. Only when she recognised the anger for what it was, could she begin to deal with it. Denial of anger can result in depression, bitterness, resentment, physical illness or even suicide.

Jesus says some hard things about those who are angry in a destructive way. He says that anger with a brother is like killing him.[23] In the parable of the prodigal son, the older son is self-righteous, showing his repressed anger by despising the younger brother who had wasted all his wealth and being angry with his father for welcoming him home.[24] Sometimes, people feel God is unfair to forgive a notorious evil-liver instead of rejoicing that he has repented. As prisoners in Rwanda are being released, many genocide survivors feel rage that they are being unfairly welcomed back into the community.

Roméo Dallaire was UN General at the time of the genocide. His anger is very evident in his book, *Shake Hands with the Devil*. Anger against those who refused him the means to stop the genocide, as well as with those who actually committed the terrible deeds. He suffered a breakdown as a result of the horrors he had witnessed and attempted suicide. He was eventually invalided out of the Canadian Army with post-traumatic stress syndrome. He is now special adviser to the Canadian government on war-affected children. He was deeply affected by the plight of the children who survived in Rwanda, most of whom saw a family member or at least someone they knew killed before their eyes. He says,

> The global village is deteriorating at a rapid pace, and in the children of the world the result is rage. It is the rage I saw in the eyes of the teenage Interahamwe militiamen in Rwanda, it is the rage I sensed in the hearts of the children of Sierra Leone, it is the rage I felt in crowds of ordinary civilians in Rwanda and it is the rage that resulted in September 11. Human beings who have no rights, no security, no future, no hope and no means to survive are a desperate group who will do desperate things to take what they believe they need and deserve.[25]

He also says that many reasons "can lead directly to a people having no hope for the future and being forced in their poverty and despair to resort to violence just to survive. This lack of hope in the future is the root cause of rage. If we cannot provide hope for the untold masses of the world then the future will be nothing but a repeat of Rwanda, Sierra Leone, the Congo and September 11."[26]

How can we deal with this anger? In the workshops on the cross in the AEE seminars, people's anger is often expressed, and carried to the cross with their pain. "Anger is often the result of deep pain in our hearts. If someone is full of anger and cannot forgive, it's because they have not found an answer for the pain they feel. Simply telling them not to be angry will not help them. Rather it only adds condemnation. What we must do is help them to bring their pain to the cross of Jesus and experience his healing."[27]

Notes

1. Not her real name
2. Nehemiah 5:6
3. Numbers 32:10–13
4. Deuteronomy 29:24–28
5. eg Amos 5:10–24
6. eg Romans 1:18; Colossians 3:5–6; 2 Thessalonians 2:8–12
7. Hebrews 10:31
8. See also the similar accounts in Matthew 21:12–13; Mark 11:15–17; Luke 19:45–46
9. Acts 5:1–11
10. Acts 8:18–24
11. Acts 13:8–12
12. All these examples come from a list of references in Lloyd with Bresser, 2001, p 79
13. Genesis 15:13–16
14. 2 Peter 3:9
15. eg Psalm 30:5; 78:38; 86:15; 103:8
16. eg Isaiah 54:8; Jeremiah 3:12; Hosea 14:4; Micah 7:18
17. Luke 6:27–28
18. See chapter 8
19. Monbourquette, 2000, p 21
20. Ibid, p 116
21. Ibid, p 111

22. Genesis 50:15–21
23. Matthew 5:22
24. Luke 15:25–32
25. Dallaire, 2003, p 521
26. Ibid, p 522
27. Lloyd with Bresser, 2001, p 80

CHAPTER TEN

Conflict resolution

"Blessed are the peacemakers, for they shall be
called sons of God" *(Matthew 5:9)*

Conflict is an inevitable part of the human condition. Lederach is convinced that it was present in the Garden of Eden because God created two human beings, each in his own image yet different from the other, and both having free will.[1] Since no two people are alike, it is important to learn how to manage conflict without it developing into strife.

> Evidence of the hardships of living together abounds: conflicts between couples, within families, between separated lovers or divorced people, between bosses and employees, between friends and neighbours, among races and nations. At some point, each of us needs to forgive in order to re-establish peace and continue living with one another. When I asked a couple who were celebrating their fiftieth wedding anniversary for the secret of their lasting happiness, the wife replied: "Never once, after quarrelling, did we go to sleep without asking each other for forgiveness."[2]

That couple had recognised the value of the old advice: "Do not let the sun go down on your anger."[3] It is still the best way of dealing with conflict.

A large part of the PHARP seminars is devoted to conflict resolution without destructive anger. "We are living in a world full of conflicts, and people have very different views of those conflicts. To some, it is a disagreeable inconvenience that they are not willing to hear about. To others, conflict is threatening and hurting. But few people view conflict as an opportunity to solve common problems in a way that honours God and is beneficial to everyone involved in the process," says Rev Felicien Nemeyimana in the preface to the Bible Study Guide prepared by MAP International in Nairobi, which is the basis for their seminars.

In the seminars, they study how conflict was resolved in different situations in the Bible. They ask how they would have reacted in these situations. Studying biblical principles for dealing with conflict helps them understand how they can relate this to their own situations.

For example:

- When it was apparent that they had to separate because of conflict between their servants, Abraham allowed Lot to choose first which way he wanted to go. As the elder, Abraham should have had first choice, but he gave way to the other, trusting that God would be in the choice.[4]
- Joseph, on the other hand, was not prepared to betray his moral principles, even when he was accused by Potiphar's wife; he found himself in prison as a result. Rather than give in to immoral demands, he fled and accepted the false charge.[5]
- Miriam and Aaron challenged Moses's authority, apparently as a result of dissension in the home because of Moses's wife. Moses trusted God to vindicate him. When Miriam was punished with leprosy, Moses interceded for her.[6]
- For years David had been hounded by Saul; but when he found Saul asleep and at his mercy, he refused to take advantage of him or to take his revenge, respecting the authority of the king.[7]

Often when we are hurt, our instinct is to hit back. These examples show how conflict can be resolved in better ways. Not defending our rights, but allowing others to win where no principles are involved, may sound wimpish but can often lead to cessation of conflict. Where moral principles are involved, the only way is to stand firm. This is illustrated by the way Paul confronted Peter when he saw him reneging on his principles and breaking table-fellowship with Gentiles.[8] Obviously that conflict was resolved, though we are not told how, because at the Council of Jerusalem, Peter supported Paul and Barnabas in their work amongst the Gentiles. The people there, after heated debate, were silent and listened.[9] How important it is to listen to each other! It is also important to listen to God. Praying for the one who harmed us can move us forward on the path to forgiveness, however hard that might be. Sometimes it changes attitudes – either ours or theirs – so that we do not to seek revenge. Henri Lacordaire said, "Do you want to be happy for a moment? Then seek revenge. Do you want to be happy for ever? Then grant forgiveness."[10]

Life is full of conflicts, and we need to seek ways of resolving them without revenge. Monbourquette says, "The instinct for revenge blinds anyone who gives in to it. How can someone determine precisely the exact amount of their suffering in order to exact equivalent suffering from the perpetrator? In truth, the offender and the victim get involved in an endlessly escalating exchange in which it becomes more and more difficult to judge that the blows are equivalent."[11] Or again, "The satisfaction that revenge provides is short-lived. It cannot compensate for the damage it produces in the network of human relationships. Furthermore, revenge triggers cycles of violence that are hard to break. An obsession with revenge contributes nothing to healing the victim's wounds, but instead makes them worse."[12]

The truth of these words has been amply demonstrated in

Rwanda and in the Middle East with the constant revenge killings between Hutu and Tutsi or between Israel and Palestine. Someone has to take the first step in seeking space for antagonists to listen to each other and find ways to defuse the situation.

John Paul Lederach has spent more than 20 years in reconciliation ministry, visiting many countries in conflict around the world. He says that "one of the least-understood aspects of reconciliation is how to think about and allow for spaces of separation as an acceptable stage in the spiritual journey toward reconciliation".[13] He discusses the story of Jacob and Esau, two brothers with a history of deception and anger. Jacob tricks Esau out of his blessing as the birthright of the older son. You can hear the anguish in Esau's cry, "Bless me, me also, O my father!" This soon turns to anger and hatred, and Jacob has to flee for his life.[14]

After years of separation from his family, now with wives, children and wealth, God told him to return to the land of his birth. The closer to home, the more fearful Jacob became, until he heard that Esau was coming to meet him with 400 men. He cried out to the God who had told him to return, "Deliver me, I pray from the hand of my brother, from the hand of Esau; for I fear him, lest he come and attack me and the mother with the children."[15] Jacob's consciousness of his own guilt had led him to fear the one whom he had wronged. That night he had an encounter with God and was brought to acknowledge who he was – Jacob, the striver, the supplanter. God blesses him and gives him a new name, Israel. Still limping from this encounter, he meets his brother and instead of the hatred he had feared, he is met with an embrace. He says, "I have seen your face as though I had seen the face of God."[16]

In his fear and guilt, Jacob had built a bogeyman, dehumanising Esau. Now in the personal encounter, he recognises him as a human being, made in the image of God like him. Lederach says, "Fear and bitterness are rooted in the experi-

ences we have had with others. The journey toward reconciliation always involves turning toward the people who have
contributed to our pain. As in the case of Jacob, it means turning toward the enemy. There are two important changes during Jacob's journey. First, he turns toward Esau. Second, he
seeks the face of his brother. It is impossible for us to make
significant progress on the journey of reconciliation without
these two elements."[17]

But first had come the period of separation. Then the decision to turn back, in fear, yes, but also with a desire to make
reparation. Finally, in seeking his brother's face in a personal
encounter, Jacob sees the face of God.

Another story of separation is the bitter dispute between
Paul and Barnabas over John Mark, who had deserted them on
their first missionary journey.[18] Barnabas, the encourager,
wanted to give him a second chance, but to Paul the mission
was all-important, and he did not want to risk being let down
a second time. In conflict between people-oriented and task-
oriented people, often, as here, the only solution is to separate, at least for a time. The young failure obviously profited
from his time with Barnabas, because towards the end of his
life, knowing that he was soon to die, alone in his prison cell,
Paul wrote to Timothy, "Get Mark and bring him with you, for
he is useful to me for ministry."[19]

In a healthy relationship, we may be able to face disagree-
ments and problems, sitting down together to attempt to
solve them. Lederach helpfully explores the various changes
that take place in our thinking, when we move from friendship, or neutrality, to viewing someone as an enemy:[20]

1 When an argument becomes heated, our thinking can
   change. Instead of viewing the issue, we see the person as
   the problem, and become antagonistic.
2 When the issue is raised we can counter by raising a different issue, which diverts attention from the problem. As

conflict develops, issues multiply, until it is hard to distinguish the real issue.

3 As conflict deepens, language changes and we project our irritation on the other, stereotyping them until our attitude becomes, "That is the way they are."

4 Now, instead of talking to the person directly, we start talking to like-minded people about them, reinforcing the stereotype, and reinforcing our own views. This is particularly true in cultures where direct confrontation is unacceptable.

5 Consideration moves away from the issue to reaction to what the other side has done. Whereas before, we wanted to understand the issue in dispute, now in increasing hostility we want to gain the upper hand over the other side, either psychologically or by violence.

6 There tends to be little or no communication between the two groups, each only talking to their own side.

After the genocide, Beatrice only wanted to speak to other Tutsi. She blamed Hutu for all the ills she had ever suffered. She grew up in Kiramuruzi, where their political officer was fanatically anti-Tutsi. Most of her relations had been killed or had fled in 1959, and she felt different from her friends who had large extended families. In 1994, almost all the Tutsi in the area were wiped out, including her parents, friends and neighbours. She heard that her beloved father had been beaten to death, a brother was drowned, others cut to pieces. Her house and their cows were destroyed. By a miracle she and her four younger brothers and sisters managed to survive and at 27, she found herself in charge of a family, with no home and no way of providing for them. The situation was made worse when two of her father's sisters arrived from Uganda with no means of support and expected her to care for them. She had never learned how to cultivate, but if she wanted food she had to learn quickly. She never expected to find happiness again and was functioning as an automaton, with no emotion except the hatred which consumed her. "I spoke nicely to Hutu," she said, "but in my mind I pictured them being beaten to death or cut to pieces. I wanted to start a group with the intention of killing as many Hutu as I could."

In 1997, she married a Tutsi soldier but was completely indifferent to him. "I refused to follow him in his postings," she said. "I was relieved when he was away, so that I had time to think about my losses and dwell again and again on how they had died. Even when my first two babies were born, I had no room in my heart for anything but hatred and my sense of loss. Outwardly I was coping but in my heart I kept thinking, 'If only I had not lost my parents, life would not be so hard', and I would start hating Hutu again."

Beatrice had two visitors from the Anglican church in Kiramuruzi who spoke to her about God. She enjoyed their visits but after they were gone the questions came back. "Is God really love? Could he possibly love me and allow all this to happen?" Sometimes her visitors spoke of forgiveness, but her heart was too full of pain and anger for this to be entertained even for a moment. They also told her that all sin was the same before God. "How can this possibly be true?" she asked herself. "Is my hatred, which has not resulted in action, the same as their killing?"

Towards the end of 2000, her husband developed asthma and resigned from the army. They moved to Byumba where it is colder, with less dust to affect him. To her horror, her house was very near the prison where the killers from her home area were confined. She used to stand where she could watch them, feeling angry that they were alive when so many of her loved ones were dead.

They were living next door to a church, and soon began to attend. Beatrice rejected the message that all sin was the same, and that God loved all people in the same way, but still was attracted by the Christians. She fell ill and found that both

Hutu and Tutsi believers came to pray for her. Although she thought that the Hutu were secretly gloating over her, their prayers were answered, and she recovered.

One day, she asked God to teach her to love again. Over the next few days, much of what she had been hearing began to make sense. "I realised that I was a sinner after all," she said. "I may not have killed but I had certainly dwelt on the thought of killing and had pictured myself killing Hutu in different ways. I had not stolen but was very pleased when I heard that a Hutu had been robbed. I began to realise that there was no good in me and threw myself on God's mercy. I told Jesus that I would follow him and see if it worked out."

Next day, to prove to herself that God had accepted her and that she no longer hated, she went to the prison and asked to see the man who had beaten her father to death. When he saw her he started back but she greeted him as an old neighbour. He put out his hand to shake hers but she said, "No, we have not seen each other for so long", and flung her arms round him in the traditional Rwandan greeting. She asked him, "Why do you think I have come to see you?"

"I don't know," he replied.

"I have been told that you are one of those who beat my father. I have not come to accuse you. I've come to tell you that I forgive you, as God has forgiven me."

He accused someone else of having beaten her father, saying that he and a friend had found him, broken and bleeding, and had stoned him to death. Beatrice quickly prayed, "Lord, help me not to picture this." She realised that the man wanted her to accuse this other man because he was angry that he was still free, but she refused to take action and never even told her family his name. She gave her father's killer 200 francs, all the money she had, and told him that she lived nearby. If he ever had any problems she told him to send a message and she would help in any way she could. She would have removed her father's name from his dossier but she learned that he was accused of several killings, so let it stand. He was taken to court and sentenced without letting her know and she never learned what had happened to him.

She took to visiting prison almost daily, slipping her former friends small sums of money or food whenever she could spare them. "I began to see their pain," she said. "Many were asking why they had done it. What was the point? I realised that God sees everything. He saw the killers, and knew them as refugees. When they returned, their houses were restored to them by the government but ours had been destroyed. Although they were in prison now, they would eventually be released. They were alive but my loved ones were dead. I found that this no longer caused me pain. I saw that it was between them and God, not between me and them."

After a time, she heard that some of the prisoners were suspicious of her acts of kindness and had accused her to the prison governor as a spy on behalf of genocide survivors only wanting to get evidence against them. She felt betrayed and angered, feeling that her efforts were wasted. Realising that she was falling into the darkness of hatred again, she attended a PHARP seminar, where she met other women, both Tutsi and Hutu. As they studied the Bible together, she felt that every word was directed at her, reassuring her of God's love and comforting her. She listened to the stories of the other women there, accepting for the first time that some Hutu had suffered as much as she had. She found those meetings were a lifeline of support as the women shared their stories, and poured out their love and forgiveness to each other.

She also went to a seminar run by AEE in Byumba. When she heard Anastase standing in the gap on behalf of Tutsi, asking for forgiveness for what they had done to Hutu, she felt that she too must stand with him and ask for forgiveness for her feelings of hatred. "I cannot say how much both PHARP and AEE have helped me," she said. "I thank God that I am released from that darkness and hatred." In 2003 she had another child. "At last I can enjoy a baby," she said, "and I am now free to love my older children as well. I can now enjoy them and my husband. Before I had no room for anything in my heart except hatred."

For conflict to be resolved there must be a decision from one side to turn, as we saw in the story of Jacob and Esau. This will involve painful decisions, and may be misunderstood by our own group. Beatrice decided to put into action her forgiveness by visiting her father's killer, and helping her school friends despite the accusations she suffered. It was as she relinquished her stereotypes and began to see Hutu as people, many of whom had suffered as she had, that she was able to forgive. In the seminars there was space, where Hutu and Tutsi alike listened to each other and learned to pray for each other.

Lederach has found that a key verse in seeking reconciliation is Psalm 85:10, which in his Spanish translation reads: "Mercy and truth have met together; Justice and peace have kissed."[21] In his workshops he often splits the groups into four, and asks each group to treat one of the above elements as a person, thinking about what each would say in a particular situation.

1 Without truth there can be no resolution of conflict. Truth validates wrongs suffered, enabling people to hear both sides of the question, but on its own it leaves people feeling vulnerable.
2 Mercy is willing to forgive and accept people, wanting a new start. It encompasses the idea of grace, but it can be too quick to move on, covering over deep wounds without dealing with them properly.
3 Justice wants to right wrongs, make reparation, create equal opportunities, but can be seen to be harsh and unforgiving.
4 Peace brings feelings of harmony, well-being and security, but if this is achieved for some at the expense of others, it is a false peace.

"Truth is the longing for acknowledgement of wrong and the validation of painful loss and experiences, but it is coupled with Mercy, which articulates the need for acceptance, letting go, and a new beginning. Justice represents the search for individual and group rights, for social restructuring, and for restitution, but it is linked with Peace, which underscores the need for interdependence, well-being and security."[22] Only where all four meet together can there be a place for true reconciliation.

One of the most important tasks of a peace-builder is to listen, and to help others to listen to each other. Storytelling is very powerful in the resolution of conflict. Before the South African elections in 1994, African Enterprise, South Africa, had done much to pave the way for reconciliation by inviting leaders from the different political parties to a game lodge.[23] Everyone who came had to be prepared to tell his life story and the others to listen. As they heard the traumas of others which had led them to take up the political positions they had, many said, "I did not realise that you, too, had suffered."

Everyone working for reconciliation in Rwanda makes time for stories to be told across ethnic divides. They are concerned that people should listen to each other. A Tutsi will often say, "I didn't realise that the Hutu also suffered in the war." As they listen to one another, the way is paved towards reconciliation. Often, hearing the stories of the killers enables victims to forgive. Helping people to listen to each other's stories and to understand the background to the killings, can lead both Hutu and Tutsi to ask for forgiveness on behalf of their people for what led up to the killings. They see each other as they are, and not as the stereotypes they had imagined. Truth leads to mercy as they forgive each other, and reconciliation follows, although justice may still need to be seen to be done in the community for true peace to result.

Notes

1. Lederach, 1999, pp 112–17. See chapter 2
2. Monbourquette, 2000, p 19
3. Ephesians 4:26 (RSV)
4. Genesis 13:1–18
5. Genesis 39:1–23
6. Numbers 12:1–16
7. 1 Samuel 24:1–22
8. Galatians 2:11–14
9. Acts 15:12
10. Quoted by Monbourquette, 2000, p 19
11. Monbourquette, 2000, p 24
12. Ibid, p 25
13. Lederach, 1999, p 20
14. Genesis 27:34, 41
15. Genesis 32:11
16. Genesis 33:10
17. Lederach, 1999, p 24–25
18. Acts 15:36–39
19. 2 Timothy 4:11
20. This list is adapted from Lederach, 1999, pp 104–9
21. Most English Bibles have "righteousness" instead of "justice", but the Hebrew is the same word for both
22. Lederach, 1997, pp 28–9
23. The story is told in *The Passing Summer* by Michael Cassidy, London, Hodder & Stoughton, 1989

CHAPTER ELEVEN

Repentance + Forgiveness = Reconciliation

"Now all things are of God, who has reconciled us to himself through Jesus Christ, and has given us the ministry of reconciliation, that is, that God was in Christ reconciling the world to himself, not imputing their trespasses to them, and has committed to us the word of reconciliation." *(2 Corinthians 5:18–19)*

Repentance + Forgiveness = Reconciliation is a slogan used by PHARP in their magazine called *The Mediator*, because this is their main emphasis. A mediator is often employed in Rwanda in various contexts: to negotiate a wedding, perhaps; or to bring together two sides in a dispute. As Christians we are called to be peacemakers,[1] and have been entrusted with the message of reconciliation.[2] It is possible, though difficult, to forgive someone who has not confessed his crime and asked for forgiveness, but true reconciliation is impossible without movement on both sides, confession and repentance on the one hand, and forgiveness on the other. For this we often need a mediator. MOUCECORE,[3] frequently finds itself in the role of mediator, seeking to bring together victim and offender.

The ministry was founded before the war when, in 1993, Bishop Alexis Bilindabagabo[4] became concerned about disunity in the Anglican Church. He felt that young people were being given a bad example by their elders, and were rejecting the gospel. Together with a number of similar-minded people, he started MOUCECORE (The Christian Movement for Evangelism, Counselling and Reconciliation), whose main focus was evangelism among young people.

In October 1994, Michel Kayitaba,[5] one of the founder members, was praying about the future. He, together with his wife and five children, had been miraculously preserved through the genocide, and he felt there must be a reason that they had survived such a holocaust. He had been a secondary school teacher before the war, but now his burden was how to rebuild Rwanda and reconcile people who had been savagely divided.

As he prayed, he felt the Lord Jesus saying to him, as he had said to Peter, "I have prayed for you, that your faith should not fail; and when you have returned to me, strengthen your brethren."[6] Despite the fact that he and his wife had lost almost all of their extended family, he was not as paralysed by grief and anger as were many of his friends. He had no work, no home, no belongings, but he did have his immediate family. "I felt that this was only by God's grace," he says. "I felt that Jesus had been praying for me to be strengthened through all that had happened, so that I could strengthen my brothers and sisters in the Christian family." But how?

One day he bumped into Bishop Alexis. It was at a time when one was surprised to find a friend still alive, and they hugged each other with joyful tears. As they exchanged news, the bishop told him that he had started the Barakabaho Foundation to deal with the plight of the hundreds of orphans who had lost their parents. "Would you like to take over MOUCECORE?" he asked. Michel felt that this could be the answer to his prayers. After a further time of prayer, he was handed the legal papers of MOUCECORE.

Feeling strongly that God was calling him to strengthen the church, which was in total disarray, he knew that his emphasis would be different to that of Bishop Alexis. Many Christians had been involved in the killings; the church was blamed for what had happened, and people were saying that God was dead or had abandoned them. Michel thought that this was the church's opportunity to rebuild in a new way.

In November 1994, he had been asked to speak at a small Anglican church in Shyogwe Diocese at a place called Mwari, near Gitarama, where there had been massacres of both Hutu and Tutsi. He brought them this challenge. "What are we going to do to show that God is still alive, and to demonstrate his power to heal and reconcile? How are we going to live as the people of God without ethnic divisions? How can we demonstrate the kingdom of God on earth?"

As the demoralised Christians prayed, they began to answer the challenge. "It is not right that some of us should live in good houses when many homes have been destroyed, and people we have prayed with have nowhere to live," said one. Another said, "It is not right that we should have food when they have none."

By the end of the day, they had decided to pool their resources and to build or repair houses, which had been looted or destroyed during the war. Other houses had had their tiles removed by those seeking to rebuild their own homes. Where they were known, the Christians asked for a similar number of tiles to be given to them. A grant from Tear Fund in 1995 eventually enabled them to build or restore 44 houses. As each was finished, they went to a widow who had been too frightened to return home and was staying in cramped conditions in Gitarama, and told her to come. The house was hers.

These widows, who had been fearful of Hutu, said, "Hutu killed my family, but these people have restored my home. They are not true Hutu!" As they returned to their homes and saw the love of those who welcomed them back, the barriers of pain and anger and suspicion began to fall. Many Tutsi Christians joined the Hutu to rebuild other houses.

"As we saw the power that this had to remove fear and anger," said Michel, "we began to use it as a strategy to get people working together in other places. I searched the Bible and found strong biblical principles for what we were doing, and started seminars for Christian leaders to teach these principles."

The Tear Fund grant was originally for three years, and was only accepted by Michel on a guarantee that he would not be deflected from his God-given vision. That grant has been renewed every three years since, and has enabled many of the MOUCECORE projects to start. It has also enabled a large training centre to be built in Kigali where Christian leaders from throughout the country, from all denominations, come for seminars lasting two weeks each. They return to their areas and teach others what they have learned. Those who have been touched by the MOUCECORE vision join in Solidarity Transformation Groups, pledging themselves to live the kingdom of God in their areas.

The aims of MOUCECORE are:

- to bring people to the knowledge of Christ and to help them grow in him;
- to rebuild broken relationships and bring reconciliation to Rwanda;
- to mobilise the church to take up holistic development;
- to train in HIV/AIDS care and prevention;
- to enable the church and communities to empower the poor and needy;
- to assist vulnerable groups, especially widows and orphans.

Their main areas of activity are:

1 Training/Education: They give seminars to Christian leaders and facilitators of groups in Christian discipleship, Christian leadership, Conflict transformation, Healing and

reconciliation, Community holistic development, and HIV/AIDS care and prevention.

2 Christian community mobilisation: They mobilise and enable small groups of volunteer burden-bearers among the Christian communities for the practical expression of their faith towards genocide survivors and HIV/AIDS victims. These groups provide care and support to needy people of any faith or none.

3 Small projects support: They provide revolving funds to support income-generating projects for vulnerable people, particularly in agricultural and animal husbandry activities and other projects like handicrafts.

4 Magazine: They publish a magazine called *Ngwino nawe*, meaning "You come as well", in which they publish some of their teaching material, testimonies of those who have been helped, articles on holistic development and awareness of God's creation, etc.

5 Children and youth ministries: They train Sunday School teachers, teach HIV/AIDS prevention, peace and reconciliation amongst children and hold youth camps and have Bible clubs for children.

6 Networking with other organisations: Their aim is to work in collaboration and partnership with other organisations working with a similar focus to rebuild Rwanda.

7 The Peace-building Centre: This building in Kigali offers accommodation for seminars for facilitators of the groups and for Christian leaders, as well as a guest house for visitors.

8 Advocacy: They give legal help for the poor, marginalised and oppressed.

Above all, their aim is to enable the church to live as the kingdom of God on earth, and to play its part in the healing and transformation of Rwanda. The following story has been published in their magazine.

One day in February 2004, two people went to Nyanza

prison to tell of their experiences in the genocide and to urge
the prisoners to confess and trust in the government procedure
to allow them to come out of prison soon. One was Edith,[7]
whose husband, several children and the aunt who had brought
her up had been killed in the genocide; the other, Tito, was the
man who had confessed to killing her beloved aunt, Doris.

Tito had become a Christian believer through Doris in
1984, and was a close friend of Edith. He had grown in the
faith and became a church teacher. At a time of increasing tension between Hutu and Tutsi, he fell in love with a Tutsi girl
and wanted to marry her. His Hutu family were bitterly
opposed to the match, but the church family prayed and eventually, in 1991, despite continuing opposition from his family,
they married, with Edith standing as sponsor for the bride. "I
could see no difference between our people," Tito said. "I
knew that Jesus died for all, and that he is our peace, bringing
peace to us all, Hutu and Tutsi alike."

In 1994, when the carnage started, many Tutsi fled to his
home for temporary refuge before moving on. After the death
of her father, Yvette, Edith's daughter, took refuge with them
as did several other Tutsi children. One day the soldiers came
and demanded to know where the parents of those children
were. Tito said that he did not know. He and his wife were
taken to police headquarters and told that they would be
killed, but they kept silent. "By a miracle, the soldier who was
supposed to kill us let us go," he said. They returned to the
uncertainty of their home.

Arrested again, he was asked how he had escaped. "You
must tell us where the parents of these children are. They are
cockroaches and must be stamped out." Again he kept silent,
but was taken to the barriers where he watched people killed,
before being allowed home again. While he was away, Doris
fled to his home for refuge. She stayed for about a week. "It
was such a comfort to have her there, and we prayed together
about the situation," he said.

For the third time, on 7th May 1994, a gang of killers came. This time, Tito was caught outside his house. To his horror, they brought Doris to him and ordered him to kill her. "I will never forget how awful it was," he said. "I had been taught not to fear those who could kill the body but rather the soul, but that day an uncontrollable fear seized me, and I feared men rather than God. At first I refused when they handed me a club, but then out of that fear, I hit her twice on the head. An *interahamwe* finished her off. I sank to the ground and they beat me. I thought they would kill me anyway, but the leader called them off. 'He is one of us now, leave him alone.' I was ordered to bury her, where we were, below the house."

When he returned to the house, he told his wife that the killers had taken Doris, and that she was dead. "But from that moment I had no peace and no strength. I could not forget what I had done. I prayed for mercy. The Lord told me that I was forgiven but I doubted this. How could I be forgiven?"

They learned that the RPF were a short distance away, and all the Hutu fled to a camp which had been set up by the French. In August they returned home, and shortly afterwards Edith came back. Tito continued as a catechist, teaching in the parish. There was no pastor, so he was the senior church leader, but it was as if a cancer was eating at his soul.

"In December the Holy Spirit started to tell me that I needed to confess what I had done, but how could I? When I thought of telling my wife or Edith, my godmother, I couldn't do it." For two years, he battled with his conscience. In 1997, he was sent to start another parish where he did not see Edith daily, and he could pretend it had never happened. In July 1999, he spent time alone with God, and was suddenly filled with the Holy Spirit. "That was when I was given the courage to confess," he said. After three days fasting and praying, he set out to find Edith. Three possible courses of action were open to him. He could go to the police station and confess; he would probably be killed. He could confess his guilt publicly, but he could not face the shame of the church's reaction, as he was their leader. As he prayed, he felt the Holy Spirit telling him to go for a third option, that of telling Edith and his own wife together.

He set off filled with courage, but as he drew near, that courage oozed away and he was again filled with fear. He returned home, but could neither eat nor talk. He spent another three days in prayer, and again felt able to tell Edith, but at that moment was summoned to a church meeting at Shyogwe, where he realised all he would lose. He returned home, but had no peace. "Once more I prayed, and this time God said, 'Don't hesitate; sweep it clean.' I asked again for strength and this time went with my wife to Edith's home, on 16th September 1999."

They were welcomed in as usual, and asked to spend the night. Over the meal, with the children there, he was very quiet, but after they had prayed for the night and the children had gone to bed, he said he must talk to them. "I said, 'I was one of those who destroyed your family. I killed Doris.' I asked for forgiveness. 'Send me to prison; throw me out of the family, but please forgive me.'"

Edith's first reaction was that he had gone mad. Even though she had heard rumours that he had killed Doris, she had refused to believe them, because he was such a close friend and a church leader. Tito said, "I can no longer continue to work for God with blood-stained hands." Edith said that she needed time to pray about her reaction, but his wife could not stay in the room with him. She wanted to leave him, but despite her shock, Edith said, "I watched the two of you joined together until death parts you, I cannot watch while you separate."

They returned home in an uneasy truce. Edith said that she wanted nothing to change while she prayed for the Lord's guidance, so Tito continued with his job. Edith found that she was facing many questions. If Tito could kill like that, was anyone immune? If a Christian leader like him could be a killer, was there anyone who was a true Christian? She considered the way that God had not let him alone, and the guilt and shame he had experienced over several years. Finally, his courage in coming to confess enabled her to relinquish her anger and disillusion with him. On New Year's Day 2001, over a year after his first confession, in church, Tito read Isaiah 61. The words "the year of the Lord's favour or mercy" hit Edith, and she knew that she could, indeed, forgive him. There and then, in the church, she said, "A year ago, someone told me he had killed Doris, asking for my forgiveness. I now want to tell him that in this year of the Lord's mercy, I forgive him."

Next day, Tito went to visit Edith to thank her for her forgiveness. She had not named him publicly, and he knew that the next step was still his. Again it took time to find the necessary courage, but on Pentecost Sunday, in church, he confessed what he had done, following it up with a visit to the court where he turned himself in. On 12th January 2002 he was sentenced to a year in prison, but after three months was put on a commission to visit other prisons and urge prisoners to confess, as he had done, so that they could experience the mercy of the courts. "God used my testimony," he said, "not only to bring many to confess to murder, but more importantly, to seek God's forgiveness." In February 2003, he was amongst those released by presidential decree, and he spent three months in a rehabilitation camp.

"When I was finally free to return home, even before seeing my wife I wanted to see Edith. She welcomed me home and gave me a cup of tea. We praised God together before I returned home to my wife. She had finally forgiven me, just before I testified in church. We still have no children of our own but God has given us ten orphans to care for, eight Tutsi from my wife's family and another two whom we picked up in the war. I thank God that Edith's forgiveness has led to true reconciliation."

Tito's fear in publicly confessing his sin is not surprising. It is one thing to confess to God, and know oneself forgiven; thousands have done so in prisons up and down the land. It is quite another to confess to the courts what happened. It is a different ball game entirely to go to the family of the victims and confess to them. Often a mediator needs to go with them.

There is, also, a difference between confession in the hope that a prisoner will receive a lighter sentence, and genuine repentance. Michel Kayitaba of MOUCECORE spends time teaching how to help people repent properly of their crimes. First, it is important that people face up to the truth of what they have done. Failure to do so leads to further sin, as the example of Cain[8] shows. Michel says that until people acknowledge the enormity of their crime, we need to have compassion on them and pray for them, because they cannot have peace, even though they may seem to have no problems. For years, Tito continued an outward facade of a good Christian teacher, while inwardly he was struggling to face the consequences of his actions.

Next, MOUCECORE looks at the story of Jacob, who had cheated his older brother Esau. Jacob tried to appease his brother with some of the wealth he had accumulated, but not until God wrestled with him and forced him to accept himself as he was, Jacob the schemer and supplanter, was he in a position to achieve reconciliation with Esau. Often we are surprised at the way people accept us once we have confessed our true nature, just as Esau accepted his brother.[9]

Finally, confessing before God and his people exactly what has been done and knowing that God has forgiven, leads to indescribable peace and happiness. Psalm 32 accurately describes how Tito felt before he finally confessed to murder. "When I declared not my sin, my body wasted away through my groaning all day long. For day and night thy hand was heavy upon me; my strength was dried up as by the heat of summer."[10] Confessing it to God brought relief, but the next step was to face the one who had been wronged, and ask her forgiveness with no preconditions. Tito knew that confession meant loss of his job and certain imprisonment. He was prepared for this. What he found hardest was the loss of Edith's friendship. She herself could not freely give that friendship until helped by the Holy Spirit.

Wrongdoing always has consequences. Life as it was may never be fully restored. Doris's life was gone, and cannot return in this world. Trust was broken. A friendship could have been destroyed. True repentance involved facing these consequences and asking for forgiveness, knowing that it might be withheld. In some cases, restitution for the wrong may be possible, although not usually in the case of a death.

Deborah's son was shot in 1997. She reacted by praying for her son's murderer. Some three months later, a young man came to her. "I killed your son," he said. "Take me to the authorities and let them deal with me as they will. I have not slept since I shot him. Every time I lie down, I see you praying, and I know you are praying for me." Deborah replied, "You are no longer an animal, but a man taking responsibility for your actions. I do not want to add death to death, but I want you to restore justice by replacing the son you killed. I am asking you to become my son. When you visit me, I will care for you." The young man became an adopted son in her household, taking on the duties of a son.[11]

In this case, the young man showed true repentance, not only accepting the consequences of his actions, but also being prepared to make restitution. On one occasion, a widow confessed to stealing the goat of another widow, without offering to restore the goat or to compensate in any way for its loss; she simply asked for forgiveness. It is a common practice in Rwanda to make open confession in church, but this does not necessarily show true repentance. It is possible to use such confession as a kind of one-upmanship, with no intention of making restitution or even of not repeating the sin, but simply wanting to seem a good Christian. It is only those who "confess and forsake" their sin who find mercy.[12] Matthew 3:8 says, "Bear fruits worthy of repentance." This means accepting the consequences of our actions, and seeking to make reparation. The declared aim of the *Gacaca* courts[13] is to enable killers and victims to live again in harmony, but it sometimes seems almost impossible.

Rwandans make no distinction between forgiveness and mercy; the same word, *imbabazi*, is used for both. They often think, therefore, that seeking forgiveness means that their actions will have no consequences. It is rare indeed to meet someone like Tito, who faced up to the consequences before he sought forgiveness. A Voluntary Service Overseas teacher said she was angered by her students continuing to ask for forgiveness. "I tell them that I have forgiven them, but that they must be punished. Yet they keep on begging for my forgiveness." She thought that they were asking for forgiveness, but her students were seeking mercy.

MOUCECORE helps people to forgive by considering the hurts that can result from unmet needs of the human heart. They help people to face these hurts squarely and to see their consequences, whether it is years of rejection which led to bitterness and hatred, or the deep hurts of bereavement and loss which can lead to bitterness and thoughts of revenge.

Michel Kayitaba teaches that listening to the stories of Rwanda and accepting the results of its violent history is important, as is acceptance of ethnic origins, so that people are not continually pretending to be someone they are not. However, accepting one's ethnic roots means accepting the guilt of one's people, and seeking forgiveness, standing in the gap. In Rwanda, both Tutsi and Hutu are responsible for what happened. They see God's pain in the Old Testament as he asks why no one has healed the wounds of his people, and recognise that his pain is the same today. "Is there no balm in Gilead? Is there no physician there? Why then is there no recovery for the health of the daughter of my people?"[14] They look at the answer God himself gives, "For they have healed the hurt of the daughter of my people slightly, saying, 'Peace, Peace!' when there is no peace."[15]

For too long, Rwanda has healed her hurts slightly, going through periods of apparent peace, without daring to face the deep traumas in her people which have festered before exploding into more violence. At last, following the horror of the genocide, the government, as well as Christian organisations, are facing this pain. "The purpose of teaching the history is to enable our people to accept responsibility for the wounds of our country," says Michel, "and to encourage them to take responsibility for healing those wounds." In all their seminars, they teach people from both sides of the ethnic divide how to leave behind division and work towards reconciliation.

The heart of MOUCECORE teaching is to help people to see the results of bitterness and the need to root it out. "Pursue peace with all people, and holiness, without which no one will see the Lord: looking carefully lest anyone fall short of the grace of God; lest any root of bitterness springing up cause trouble, and by this many become defiled."[16] They look at the consequences of letting bitterness take root: anger, division and, above all, a desire for revenge.

Not to take revenge must be a conscious decision. Taking revenge is to play God and usurp his powers, because he has said, not once but three times, "'Vengeance is mine. I will repay,' says the Lord".[17] Rick Warren says, "It is when we try to be like God that we end up most like Satan, who desired the same thing."[18] Taking revenge places us on the same level as the one who has wronged us. It may be satisfying for a moment, but it will not stop the hurt.

Like Michel, Monbourquette considers that the first step towards forgiving is to decide not to seek revenge. He lists the evil consequences of a thirst for revenge, all of which are harmful.[19]

These consequences include:

- Revenge focuses your attention and energy on the past. There is no space for the present and the future holds no interest.
- The spirit of retaliation keeps re-opening your wound by reminding you of the offence. You cannot enjoy the peace and calm which your wound needs to scar over and heal.
- To satisfy your desire for revenge, you will have to imitate your offender, in spite of yourself, and let yourself be dragged into their infernal cycle. Not only will you hurt yourself more, but you will also demean yourself in the process.
- Punishing someone for the sheer pleasure of revenge will arouse deep feelings of guilt in you. You will feel guilty for using another person's suffering to relieve your own humiliation.
- Revenge will fuel your resentment, hostility and anger, all feelings that generate stress, [...] and stress-related diseases.

It is not easy, however, to decide not to take revenge when the offender is unrepentant and may be living without any apparent consequences. A skit used in the AEE seminars is very powerful. One person pretends to harm another, who refuses to forgive. They tie a rope to the wrists of both people. Wherever the injured one goes, he takes the other with him. As soon as he forgives, he ties his end of the rope to a wooden cross, symbolically transferring his pain from the injury to Jesus. He is set free to rejoice. The one who committed the sin is now bound to the cross and under the judgement of God. He will remain there, unless and until, in his turn, he repents and transfers his sin to Jesus. Then he too is free.

Like the Psalmist, we can be near to slipping when we see those who have harmed us prosper. Like him, we need to see that God will hold them responsible. "When I thought how to understand this, it was too painful for me — until I went into the sanctuary of God; then I understood their end."[20] It is not for us to play God and take revenge. Unless the one who has harmed us repents of his sin and seeks God's mercy, his end is too awful to contemplate. God can enable us to pray for that mercy.

Gerald Sittser's family were killed by a drunken driver who was later acquitted by the courts. He spent hours fantasising about horrible situations in which the driver suffered as he, Sittser, was suffering.

> I wanted to punish the wrongdoer and get even. The very thought of forgiveness seemed abhorrent to me. I realised at that moment that I had to forgive. If not, I would be consumed by my own unforgiveness ... I think I was spared excessive preoccupation with revenge because I believe that God is just, even though the judicial system is not. Ultimately every human being will have to stand before God, and God will judge every person with wisdom and impartiality. Human systems may fail; God's justice does not. I also believe that God is merciful, in ways that far exceed what we could imagine or muster ourselves. It is the tension between God's justice and mercy that makes God so capable of dealing with wrongdoers. God is able to punish people without destroying them, and to forgive people without indulging them.[21]

Having decided not to take revenge, the next step is to recognise that Jesus carried our pains as well as our sins on the cross. In their seminars, MOUCECORE concentrate on the cross and transfer the pain to Jesus, though they seldom use a physical cross, as AEE do. Only when the depth of their pain has been recognised and dealt with, can people be helped to see that it is possible to forgive.

In 2004 in a great venture of faith, AEE began running seminars for survivors of the genocide and released prisoners. At first they were very difficult, with deep suspicion on both sides, but after the Cross Workshop, these attitudes changed.

This was often the first opportunity that these people had had to sit with each other and to listen to their stories, to realise that they were all on the same journey.

As victims listened to the sufferings of the prisoners, their hearts melted. "We didn't understand. We thought the Hutu were gloating over what they had done. We hadn't realised that they also had deep pain." Often the stories of the prisoners include the deaths of loved ones though malnutrition as their wives struggled to keep going without husbands. Frequently they gave up the struggle, were taken on by other men, and made new lives for themselves. Often they had other children, and the prisoners were left alone. The anguish of their guilt as they consider what they have done frequently touches the victims' hearts. "We didn't realise that they really were sorry. We thought they were manipulating the system in confessing, hoping to be released sooner, but now we see that their tears are genuine."

At one such seminar in March 2004, a released prisoner, Philip,[22] told his story. He was a Hutu who had been taught by his grandmother to hate Tutsi. Throughout his childhood she fed him stories of their arrogance and the ways they had humiliated Hutu, often beating and killing them indiscriminately under the old monarchy. When he became a Christian he thought that he had put this hatred behind him, but the propaganda put out by the government and over the radio rekindled the hatred fed to him by his grandmother, so that he joined the *interahamwe* and started killing.

Afterwards, he returned to Kigali, but knew that he was on the wanted list. He kept on the move, always one step ahead of the soldiers who were hunting him. He could not forget what he had done. Indeed, he could not understand how he could have done it. He described himself as a former Christian who had put himself beyond the reach of God's mercy. Voices inside his head were driving him mad: "What about the babies you killed? What harm had they done you? Were those old women a danger to you?" He could not sleep, and started to take drugs to silence his voices, all the time driven by fear to keep on the move.

One night in 1995, he started to weep. He poured out his guilt before God and begged his forgiveness. A supernatural peace filled his heart, and he decided to stop running and wait for the police to arrest him. "I wanted to face justice," he said, "even though I knew it would mean the death sentence. I had finished running." When the police caught him and took him in for questioning, he asked them what cases they had against him. He confessed to them all, adding others that they had not heard about. In prison, he asked God to prepare him for the death sentence, knowing that he deserved it, but because of his full confession he was sentenced to life imprisonment.

After nine years, he was released to do community service. "I was happy to be released," he said, "but very fearful about returning home. How could I face the families of those I had killed?" Back in the community he was shunned by everyone, even those in church. In the seminar he wept as he told the details of what he had done, shuddering at the horror, unable to relate that killer to the person he now was. Some of the families of those he had killed began weeping too. They came to him and hugged him in forgiveness.

After that seminar, they formed a Christian Solidarity Group to act as mediator, going with him to other relations, telling his story and pleading with them to forgive.

Repentance on one hand, forgiveness on the other, together bring true reconciliation and a hope for this land still mourning for the thousands who were killed.

Notes

1. Matthew 5:9
2. 2 Corinthians 5:18–21
3. MOUCECORE (*Mouvement Chrétien pour l'Evangelisation, le Counselling et la Réconciliation*)

4. His story is told in *Rescued by Angels*, Bilindabagabo, Acorn Press, 2001

5. His story can be read in *Rwanda: The Land God Forgot?* pp 247–8 or *Faith under Fire*, Rutayisire, pp 36–45.

6. Luke 22:32

7. Her story is told in *Rwanda: The Land God Forgot?*, pp 233–5

8. Genesis 4

9. Genesis 32:13 – 33:15

10. Psalm 32:3–4 (RSV)

11. Deborah's story is taken from the World Vision Australia video "Rwanda's Gift to the World"; I have their permission to use it.

12. Proverbs 28:13

13. See chapter 7 for a fuller discussion of the *Gacaca* courts

14. Jeremiah 8:22

15. Jeremiah 8:11

16. Hebrews 12:14–15

17. Deuteronomy 32:35–36; Romans 12:19; Hebrews 10:30

18. *The Purpose Driven Life*, Zondervan, Grand Rapids, Zondervan 2002, p 79

19. Monbourquette, 2000, p 78

20. Psalm 73:16–17

21. Sittser, 1995

22. Not his real name

Epilogue

On 7th April 2004, I joined Wilberforce and his family at the two family graves I had visited nine years earlier. Each expressed a confidence that he or she was going to heaven through faith in the death of Jesus. They were confident that they would meet their loved ones again one day.

It was a day of sorrow, and of some anger at unfeeling people who say that they should forgive and forget. How could such anguish be forgotten? Two days later would be Good Friday, when we remember the death of Jesus. Not only did he carry our sins, he carried our sorrows. Only as we let him heal the deep wounds can we find the strength to forgive. Standing in the gap as a white, I asked their forgiveness for the way the Western world left Rwanda to its fate. I reminded Wilberforce of the day when he had first shown me those graves and had cried, "How do I forgive those who are not repentant? If I do, it merely releases them to do it again." We need to forgive for our own sake, so that the roots of bitterness and desire for revenge do not ruin our lives. God does not forget what happened ten years ago. He weeps with us. When we forgive, we place the wrongdoer firmly in his hands, for his justice or his mercy, as he sees fit.

As the stories recounted here are multiplied throughout the land, let us pray that the bitter cycle of revenge will cease, and there will be true reconciliation. May Rwanda be a beacon of hope to our troubled world, as God restores the years the locusts have eaten.

Hymn composed and sung by a choir at Muyumbu Church, Byumba Diocese on 8th February 2004

1 I am looking towards that country of beautiful love that is beyond the sun.
I feel tired and I have a question: When will I get there?
People of this world make me feel weak when they say,
"It is too hard, you will never make it."

Refrain
When you feel tired and heavy-laden, have patience and endure;
Remember that the fruit of blessing comes from the tree of hard work.
Be encouraged, beyond these problems, in that new country of joy the citizens love one another.
There is no separation of tribe there;
No Tutsi, no Hutu, no white, no black,
There is only love and joy.

2 In that beautiful country of love, no one is able to kill his neighbour.
In that beautiful country of love, there is no sound of gun-fire.
In that beautiful country of love there is only peace and joy.
I hope that you and I will get there.

Refrain

When you feel tired and heavy-laden, have patience and
  endure;
Remember that the fruit of blessing comes from the tree of
  hard work.
Be encouraged, beyond these problems, in that new country
  of joy the citizens love one another.
There is no separation of tribe there.
No Tutsi, no Hutu, no white, no black,
There is only love and joy.

3 Look at the Son of God.
  What brought him to our sinful and accursed world?
  He allowed himself to be nailed to the cross.
  He carried all our sins.
  It was because he wanted me and you to follow him and
    to bring us joy.
  We will live with him in peace;
  No further problems, no weariness, no separation of
    hearts with him;
  No sickness nor even death.
  We will be with him in joy.
  When we get there we will be hugged by our Lord Jesus
    and there will be such joy.
  When we get there we will hug all our friends we have
    lost.
  We will sing songs of victory and Jesus will receive all the
    glory.

As this hymn shows, Rwandans still have the horrors of the
genocide on their minds, but they hope for a time when it will
all be in the past. I pray that what they sing about for the
future may become a present reality in this beautiful country
of Rwanda.

In the body of this book the stories have been told of how each Christian agency started. In chapter 5 the story was told of the beginning of the AEE Healing and Reconciliation programme. But what about AEE itself?

AEE is the East African name for African Enterprise, which was begun in South Africa by Michael Cassidy with the expressed purpose of reaching the cities of Africa for Christ. In Rwanda the Team Leader, Israel Havugimana, had worked tirelessly for peace following the invasion of the RPF into Rwanda in 1990. He was one of the first to be killed after the president's plane was shot down at the start of the genocide in 1994. Following the war his close friend Antoine Rutayisire then took over as Team Leader in Rwanda.

Antoine had been working with the International Fellowship of Evangelical Students (IFES) before the war. (His story is told in *Faith under Fire*, pp 24–30 and pp 105–108, which I quote in chapter 3, and he is writing his autobiography.) In 1994, having been rescued by the RPF in Kigali, he was taken with his family to a displaced persons camp in Byumba where he did what he could to minister to his fellow-survivors. The chairman of IFES, hearing that he was still alive, sent a representative to him in May 1994 while the fighting was still going on. IFES offered him a ticket and a scholarship in Britain.

Antoine asked for time to pray but felt the Lord saying to him, "I want you to stay with your people, suffer with them. Live with them and minister to them." A friend wrote to him at that time, quoting 2 Corinthians 1:3 and saying, "Maybe the Lord is going to use you in the healing of this land."

As he prayed about the future, those words returned. He had been working with World Vision in the camp and when the war was over, he helped them to set up their Kigali office. They offered him a job but he said that the Lord was calling him to something other than administration. He was asked to set his vision down on paper and they would see if they could support it. From his own experience he knew that healing and forgiveness would only come through the cross. As he was still working out what he could write, he was approached by AEE to become their Team Leader in Rwanda. He knew immediately that this was right. Their vision of evangelism was what he had been coming to understand – "to preach the gospel in word and deed".

His experience as an orphan had taught him how easy it was to blame those who had killed his father for all his problems. He also knew that physical needs prevented inner wounds from healing, so his first priority was to meet the immediate needs of the survivors. But he also knew that those inner wounds were kept raw by anger and the pain of loss, so another important priority was to seek means of healing and reconciliation by means of preaching the cross.

Evangelism by deed

1 Initially AEE set up a child care centre in Butare to care for the hundreds of orphans or abandoned children. One story summarises the situation they found. A grenade had gone off near a family fleeing for their lives. A child was badly injured in the blast. Her parents knew they would have to run and she would hold them up. AEE took her in and arranged for

her to be treated. Years later she was able to walk again but is still unable to forgive her parents for abandoning her.

2 By the end of 1995, AEE realised that the 207 children needed more individual care than could be provided by the hard-pressed staff. The very atmosphere of the orphanage was keeping alive the memory of what they had lost and adding to the depression of the children. So they developed a child/family support programme. They managed to place the majority of their children with relatives who had survived the genocide, and others were adopted by AEE staff or other Christians. These children were visited regularly and money provided to help in their schooling.

3 They also began a widows' programme, initially helping with basic needs such as blankets and cooking utensils as well as rice and beans for food. Later they helped rebuild the widows' homes and later still, provided micro-credit schemes whereby widows could begin to earn their own living.

Ten years later these initial programmes have developed into community development programmes in which widows and orphans are enabled to improve their own circumstances. There is also a large HIV/AIDS programme and support for child-headed households.

Evangelism by word

1 At first Antoine concentrated on survivors, knowing that it was the message of the cross that had brought him to forgive those who had killed his father years before. AEE started holding large meetings in every town where they preached about the saving power of the cross and asked people to give testimonies about how they had been enabled to forgive. In 1995 there was a huge mission in Kigali at which Michael Cassidy, Bishop Desmond Tutu and others were the speakers.

2 They started a radio programme, which still goes out nationwide, preaching on forgiveness and reconciliation.

3 At an early meeting in 1994, he met Dr Rhiannon Lloyd of Mercy Ministries International and saw her emphasis on the cross and her desire for healing and reconciliation. Rather than do this work himself, he encouraged her; eventually the healing and reconciliation programmes which have been described in detail in chapter 5 became part of the AEE programme. These seminars were held amongst the children in the AEE child support programmes, amongst widows and even with the AEE staff, as well as with church leaders throughout the country.

4 In 1995 with Michael Cassidy, Antoine visited Kigali prison. For the first time it dawned on him that these people also needed to hear the message of the cross. Someone had said to him, "Why visit those killers? They deserve to rot in Hell!" As he looked at the prisoners, he knew that they needed the chance to confess and that there was no real hope of reconciliation unless there was movement on both sides. Repentance and forgiveness together bring reconciliation. He and his staff visited all the prisons in the country over the following years. Sometimes Antoine visited a prison three times a week, preaching the vital message of the healing power of the cross. When prisoners were released by presidential decree in 2003, the AEE team did all they could to encourage the churches to get involved in welcoming the prisoners home. The healing and reconciliation regional teams also held seminars to bring reconciliation between the survivors and the killers. As part of their prison ministry AEE are encouraging church leaders to get fully involved in the *Gacaca* process.

5 Prayer backs all they do. Every year they spend the week between Christmas and the New Year seeking God's will for the coming year. In 1996, they felt led to pray for the return of the refugees without bloodshed. To the wonder of

the world, it happened. In 1997, Antoine felt God telling him to go to Ruhengeri and pray for the fighting there to cease. The Ruhengeri area was still very unstable, with killings every week both of Tutsi and Hutu. It was unsafe for Tutsi to travel there and Antoine knew that they would be viewed with suspicion and fear by the majority Hutu. Nevertheless, he went with a mainly Tutsi team. He told his own story as a Tutsi survivor from 1973 as well as 1994. He then introduced his team who were all returned refugees from Uganda, Tanzania, Congo and Burundi who had been exiled since 1973. As expected there was a lot of suspicion but Antoine heard the Lord say, "Be open to them, tell them the truth. It is my business how they respond." As the team members heard of all the hardships and deaths in the area, they began to weep. A Hutu said, "When we saw you weeping over our misfortunes, we realised that you were genuine and we began to listen to your message." Antoine realised that if there was going to be true reconciliation it could only happen through prayer. Since then, the AEE team have been teaching on prayer and intercession and have set up a network of prayer cells throughout the country.

Selected case histories from four Christian organisations studied in this book

1 A case study from the AEE seminars

During Mourning Week, from 6th to 13th April 2003, when the country was remembering the start of the genocide on 7th April 1994, the National Team of AEE held a seminar in Nyamata. Noel, the chauffeur, had been teaching about the cross and how Jesus not only bore our sins but also our pains on the cross. He told the story of the pain of one woman who had been so severely injured that she had been unable to move. He described her anguish at being unable to help her children who were crying for her and who soon died. At that time and in that place it was too much. Suddenly people were moaning and screaming all over the room. Two girls ran out crying. They were followed by members of the team while Joseph and the others calmed the rest. As it became quieter, those who had run out came back.

Vestine, a Hutu, came to the front and told her story. She had been ten years old in 1994 and had been unaware of ethnic differences until the killing began, and suddenly all her friends and neighbours were either killing or being killed. Her father had died when she was young and she had been brought up by her mother. They fled when the RPF came close, and were taken to a displaced persons' camp which had been set up by the French at Kibeho. The RPF considered it a place of refuge for the killers and wanted to disperse those who were there.

Vestine's mother was old, starving and ill, lying in one of the shelters. Vestine felt helpless as she cried out for water, and tried to help her to the river. They staggered outside just as the RPF attacked the camp, and her mother was killed. Vestine still had nightmares of her mother crying for water, and when Noel had spoken of this Tutsi lady's suffering, she could not bear it and left the room. She did not think that she would be heard by the others because she was a Hutu.

It was indeed the first time that many there realised that Hutu had suffered in the same way as they had. Many gathered round Vestine and prayed for her. Later, she nailed her paper to the cross and felt the agony she had carried for years leave her. "I tried to nail my paper as close to the place Jesus's heart would have been," she said. "Others had got there first but I squeezed my paper in, knowing that he had taken my pain into his heart. Now I pray for others who have suffered as I have."

Yvette had also fled from the room that day. A Tutsi, she was amazed to hear that Hutu had also suffered. She had been twelve years old in 1994 and was severely injured in the head by those who killed her family. Her father knew that he was dying, and asked a Tutsi neighbour, who had somehow survived the massacre, to look after her. For several weeks, the two of them hid in the swamps and survived the many searches by bands of killers. When it was all over, they returned to his home in Nyamata. The young man looked after Yvette as her father had asked and managed to get her into school. When she was 16, he also got her pregnant. She had expected him to marry her, but he left her and found another woman. This betrayal on top of all she had suffered sent her mad. She left school and looked after her baby as best she could, living wild and begging for food.

At that seminar she was able to speak for the first time about what had happened to her. As they listened to her story of betrayal, many were moved to tears and asked her forgiveness for not helping her before. Yvette listened as Vestine spoke of her unbearable hurts and for the first time realised that the Tutsi were not the only sufferers. She heard Noel, a Hutu, stand weeping and ask for forgiveness on behalf of his people, accepting the guilt of all that the Hutu had done even though he had not been involved. He was among those who prayed for her, and she saw that some Hutu could be good. A few weeks later it was hard to realise that she had been considered mad. She said that she knew her pain had been nailed to the cross but she still blamed the Hutu for all that had happened to her. "I cannot imagine that I will ever be able to forgive them," she said, "but I know it is early days. God has already done so much for me, I suppose he is able to change my heart over this as well."

Today at Nyamata, a team of five Christians work together for the AEE seminars. In 1994, Rhiannon had been told that it would be impossible to hold interdenominational meetings because of the hatred and suspicion between Christians. This team includes a Roman Catholic, a Pentecostal, an Anglican, and a Seventh Day Adventist. They are travelling all over their area telling how God has healed them and enabled them to forgive their enemies, removing suspicion between them. Despite the poverty, there is renewed hope in Nyamata, as the Holy Spirit pours out his love on the people.

2 A case study from Solace Ministries

Rose[1] was born in Butare to a Tutsi family, and experienced difficulty in getting schooling because of discrimination. Her older sister went to a convent school, and eventually became a nun. She was married in 1983 at the age of 17 and soon had a child. In 1985, she had just given birth to her second baby when her husband was imprisoned on a trumped-up charge. He was taken to Kigali where, for two years, he was treated very badly. Rose developed a stomach ulcer from her worry. She began to hate all Hutu, for preventing her from learning, and for taking her husband away. He was released in 1987 but was unable to find a job until 1991. In the meantime, Rose gave birth to her third child.

In 1994 the *interahamwe* killed her husband. Her two younger children had just left the house when the killers came, and they disappeared. Believing that they had both been killed, she hid with her nine-year-old and eventually got to Kigali where the RPF had taken control. She soon learned that her parents and three of her brothers and sisters had also been killed.

In 1997, her husband's brother took her as his wife and she had another child. A few months later he was killed in Congo where he was serving as a soldier. She began meeting with counsellors from Solace Ministries who listened as she told her story. It took time to learn to trust them. She would leave it for a time and then return, but they always welcomed her. One day, a UNHCR worker told Rose that they had traced one of her missing children to Butare. Solace Ministries supported her when she said she could not face returning to Butare, the scene of so much terror. They rejoiced with her when the UNHCR worker brought the little boy to her. The two children had been separated in the crowds and he never saw his brother again. Rose believes he must have been killed.

Rose was helped by Solace Ministries to face her fears and worries for the future. They went with her to Butare to find out what had happened to her family. She found the bodies of her parents, her nun sister and other relatives and was able to bury them. "All this time, Solace was there for me," she said. "Each time of grief, I would go to Solace and talk it out, and they would pray with me. They taught me to pray and to study the Bible. At Solace, I met some Hutu who helped me. I began to realise that not all Hutu had been involved in these atrocities. Slowly my anger against them lessened. I heard one Hutu lady ask for forgiveness on behalf of her people. I could see that she grieved for what had been done. I said it was not she who had done it, and I asked for forgiveness for the bad things Tutsi had done."

Once she went to her Roman Catholic church to pray and saw a Hutu lady wearing clothes which she recognised as belonging to her aunt who had been killed. When challenged, she ran off. Rose went to Solace, where they prayed with her and someone accompanied her to look for this woman. When she found her, she told of her shock and pain at seeing her wearing her aunt's clothes. "I told her that I forgave her but wanted to ask her, as another person who prays as I do, to tell me where she found them. She asked if I would imprison her. 'No.' 'Will you report me to *Gacaca*?' 'No.' Once she was reassured that I would not report her she told me that her husband had been amongst those who looted my aunt's house after she and her five children had been killed. They had set fire to the house and the car. I was able to forgive her completely."

She also met an old woman whose two sons had put her parents down a longdrop latrine where they died. The woman tried to run away, fearing that she would be killed, but Rose followed her and told her that she had met with Jesus and would not harm her. She knew that it was the woman's children, not her, who had killed her parents, and she would not take revenge on her. They still meet each other in peace.

"Every time I come to Solace they help me to face my pain and pray for me," says Rose. "I cannot tell you how much they have helped me. As I have been helped to forgive, I have realised that I also need to seek forgiveness."

One of her neighbours was a former *interahamwe* soldier. He wanted to have a good wedding for his daughter, and arranged a big celebration at home with dancing and music. In her pain, Rose could not bear to see him happy, so she went with some friends to complain to the police about the noise. They came and spoilt his celebrations. He bought a grinding machine to earn money grinding corn for his neighbours. The same group went to complain about the noise, and he was prevented from using it. "I realised that this was a result of my hatred, so I asked his forgiveness. He had not realised that I was behind his problems, but he forgave me and we are now friends. It was terribly hard to find the courage to speak to him but I'm glad I did. I have forgiven those who falsely accused my husband and made him go through those years of imprisonment and torture. I face the *Gacaca* courts knowing that I can speak the truth. With Solace, we have been able to meet the local community leaders and I have now been asked to be one."

She has visited several other areas of Rwanda to preach and teach the Bible. She wants to tell others how God has healed her pain and how they too can find the peace she has received. "What helped me to forgive was first and foremost prayer. Everything we do at Solace is with prayer. Listening to others tell their stories and realising that Hutu also have pain has helped me. It was only as the pain in my heart subsided that I was able to forgive from a heart at rest. If we can meet with God and learn of each other's pain, this country will be healed. Sometimes as many as 500 people whose scars have been healed come together to praise God and to pray for our land.

"On one occasion in 2003 a group of *bazungu* came to one of our meetings. They asked our forgiveness for what the whites had done in bringing division in our land and indeed throughout Africa. They asked for water and knelt and washed our feet. This was a powerful picture of repentance and showed us how we too should repent and ask for forgiveness."

3 A case study from PHARP

Venantie is the wife of a pastor; both are Hutu. When the RPF invaded in 1990, her husband was away on a course. She had to take responsibility for her family, taking them for safety to a displaced persons camp where they lived for four years. After the Arusha Peace Accords were signed, she returned to her home to discover that the RPF had called the remaining Hutu to a meeting in the stadium, promising them food. Instead they threw grenades, killing hundreds, including 17 members of her family, uncles and cousins. She could not speak of her pain and anger, and the wound festered in her heart. When the genocide started in 1994, she did not take part but she was glad. This time they did not flee, and when life returned to some semblance of normality, she resumed her duties as a pastor's wife, but still she did not speak about the wound festering in her heart. It had become so that she could not bear to talk to a Tutsi or even to be in the same room with one. Eventually in 2002 she was asked as the Mother's Union representative to attend a seminar run by PHARP on Reconciliation. She went reluctantly, but felt that as a pastor's wife she could not refuse.

While there she heard a Tutsi lady stand up and tell how most of her family had been wiped out by Hutu. Another said the same. A third said, "Eighteen members of my family were killed by Hutu without cause, simply because they were Tutsi. Why should I speak to them? In fact I cannot even bear to be in the same room with a Hutu."

"Why, that lady is like me," she thought. Considering the bitterness she felt, and realising that others were in exactly the same boat, she suddenly realised that she could no longer hold onto her anger. She stood to tell her story but found she could only weep. The leader said, "Let her weep. There is obviously some deep healing going on." While she wept the rest prayed for her. Eventually she had calmed enough to say what had happened to her family. Then she said, "I want to ask for-giveness for my attitude towards Tutsi during the last few years. I have been exactly like that Tutsi lady and we have both suffered in the same way. I realise that it was not all the Tutsi who killed my family and I have been unjust in seeing them all in the same way. As a Christian I know that Jesus died to take my sin and I no longer hold onto my anger." She felt a huge burden roll from her heart. Now she no longer sees all Tutsi as killers, but recognises them as individuals made in the image of God.

Christiana was one of the Tutsi ladies who had spoken at that PHARP meeting. She had had a very good life before the war even though she was Tutsi. Her husband was one of the few Tutsi with a good job in local government and they were comfortably off with a large home and family. The genocide happened in 1994. Her commune was the only one where the local government official refused to allow any slaughter; but elsewhere her parents and two of her ten children were killed, as well as about 50 members of her extended family. One daughter was raped and died of AIDS five years later. She also found that she had to care for ten orphans from her family.

As she cared for her daughter, she was consumed by hatred for the Hutu who had done such terrible things. "I felt as if I was no longer human but lived as if I were in a cloud, seeing everyone through a mist. I considered all Hutu to be animals with no feelings of any sort and I hated them."

Her husband was now a magistrate and after her daughter's death she began campaigning on behalf of women's rights. One day she had a letter from the mayor inviting her to go to a PHARP meeting on healing and reconciliation. It was a let-ter which had been sent to leaders of all women's organisa-tions.

"I arrived at the meeting still angry and full of despair in my heart. I had been brought up as a Catholic but had never stud-ied the Bible." At the meeting they were taught from the Bible and she felt a gradual stirring in her heart. She wanted to learn more.

At the second meeting, Christiana realised that she too was a sinner but that her sin had been forgiven. Her story helped Venantie to recognise her hatred and to forgive. As she recounted her story she found that she was able to say and to mean that she had forgiven the Hutu who had killed and raped her family.

"Now I am able to see Hutu as people again," she said. "I don't know who killed my family but I no longer want revenge. I can leave them to God. If the government punishes them, that is their job, but I will not seek them out."

She now has a hunger to learn more of the love of God and to study the Bible and has joined a local Pentecostal church.

4 Kiramuruzi – a case study from MOUCECORE

About 100 km north east of Kigali is the small town of Kiramuruzi. In the years before 1994 this area had a fanatically anti-Tutsi political leader who was one of the worst killers in the genocide. He told the Hutu in the town that if they stayed at home and he found them there, they would be killed as Tutsi sympathisers. Almost every Tutsi in the area was massacred without mercy. Those who fled to the church were miraculously unharmed. Elsewhere in the country a church was not considered a safe refuge but perhaps because the RPF came so soon, the church at Kiramuruzi was inviolate. Since the RPF were not too far away when the president's plane was shot down on 6th April, they were in Kiramuruzi by the 15th and were able to rescue several Tutsi. The massacres may only have lasted a few days in that area, but they were exceptionally savage. When the RPF captured the town, there followed a mass exodus to Tanzania of Hutu fearing reprisals.

I had last visited the Anglican Parish of Kiramuruzi in 1997 when a group of women showed me with great pride how they had built a house by themselves. "There are so few men around that we have to learn to work for ourselves," they explained. For some time I had been hearing of great things that God had been doing in that area, and was fascinated to hear for myself what had been happening. I had travelled there with Patricia, a Bible teacher working with MOUCECORE, and we were warmly welcomed. Emmanuel, the MOUCECORE facilitator for the area, told us what was going on.

Immediately following the genocide, he said, there was utter despair in the area, with hundreds of widows and orphans. Old men and women had no one to help them as their families had been slaughtered. Returning refugees from Uganda or Burundi were taking over houses belonging to the Hutu who had fled, but they did not feel at home. They were strangers in their own land. Every member of the community was filled with enormous pain, and suspicion was rife. The few remaining Hutu were ashamed and fearful of reprisals. The community seemed paralysed.

Out of desperation 16 Christians, both Hutu and Tutsi from the Anglican Church, led by their pastor, Rev Cyprien, met together to pray. Added to their own pain of bereavement was the anguish that some church members had taken part in the killing. "Is God dead, as some are saying?" they asked. They prayed, "God, if you are still hearing us, what do you want us to do?" They prayed about the needs of the widows and orphans and the divisions in the community. Gradually they came to a sense of purpose that they should work together across ethnic barriers, to bring reconciliation.

At first they shared their food and clothing with those in need. They realised that they needed to help people to help themselves. Most of the banana plantations had been demolished in the orgy of killing and destruction. Twenty-two more Christians joined the original group and together they restored the plantation, planting new banana trees so that there would be food. Next they tackled the fields which had been left uncultivated for several months. Together they dug and planted them. Finally they started building houses for those whose homes had been destroyed.

At this point in 1996, Rev Cyprien went to a meeting called by MOUCECORE in Byumba. When he heard the teaching on the theme, "Good News for the Poor", he realised that what they were already doing was in line with this teaching. He spoke to Michel who promised to visit. A few weeks later Michel came and gave a MOUCECORE seminar on, "Changing ourselves and helping to change others".

They asked themselves, "Have we changed? Yes, we are working together, but we are still Hutu and Tutsi in our attitudes and thinking." They stood as Tutsi and Hutu groups, confessed their ethnic hatred as sin, and asked each other for forgiveness. From this, they formed a Christian Unity Group in which they pledged themselves to represent the true church of God in all they did.

Through the group, older members of the community have found children who help in ways their children would have, had they lived. Orphans have a variety of parents to support and advise them. This is most obvious when they marry, as the members of the group act as their parents in every way. There have been fifteen such weddings in the past few years.

The parish now has two Unity groups in the main parish centre. Four daughter churches have been planted, each with their own group. A total of 270 people have pledged themselves to work together for reconciliation in these groups. The fruit of their commitment has spread to other churches. As they were building a house for one local widow, a Catholic builder was strongly impacted. He went to his padre. "You should see the love these people have for each other," he said, "and how they are putting it into practice." As a result the padre visited the pastor and invited MOUCECORE to teach them; as a result a group of Christian Unity was formed in the Catholic community. A similar thing happened amongst the

Baptists. Groups from the different churches meet in their own denominations for teaching, but frequently work together in building for those in need.

At first they thatched the houses they had built; but when MOUCECORE saw what they were doing, they gave a grant sufficient to buy iron sheets to roof six houses. Between 2000 and 2003, the groups have been able to build and roof 23 houses from contributions from their members. This was two short of their target, but they also repaired ten others.

As they prayed for the sick, they realised that hospital bills were beyond the reach of many individuals. Wanting to do more than pray, each member initially contributed 50 francs which meant that those needing hospitalisation could be helped. Later they increased the contribution to the common purse to 200 francs a month. From this they have been able to help the needy in all sorts of ways.

Orphans (which in Rwanda include the children of widows)
The group pray for and encourage the orphans in the area and have been able to help in many practical ways. They pay school travel and equipment expenses for some; others they teach principles of cultivation and development. They pay a teacher in one of the small schools which would have closed without their help. As income-generating projects take effect, some of the parents are contributing towards this salary.

Cultivation and development
A passage that is very meaningful to them is John 2:1–11 where Jesus turned water into wine at the wedding in Cana in Galilee. They use the comparison of dead fields which they have transformed into life-giving food, turning grass into beans! Having started with two fields they now have ten and the profit from selling the produce goes into the common purse.

Everything has a purpose. From the original three cows given by MOUCECORE to obtain milk for orphans and the sick, even the manure is used to improve the soil. They now have ten cows, and the profit from selling the milk goes into the common purse. Their original banana plantation has now become ten.

The local government has given them a plot in the town where they are building a training centre from which they can sell their produce in a co-operative and hold seminars for anyone who wants to come, of any faith or none. As a result of the work of the facilitators and trainers, many have become believers and joined the groups.

They meet regularly to dig the common fields every Tuesday. Every Friday afternoon they visit the poor and sick, giving practical help where needed. In the evening they meet to pray for those who have been visited. Once a month they meet for teaching from the Bible and to give their contributions. Every third Sunday, a collection is taken up from church members for this work.

Local government

When they started, local government officials considered that what they were doing was only church business. Later, remembering the appalling massacres and seeing how unity was developing, they began to ask officials from other areas to come to see what the church was doing. In recognition of what has been achieved, local government has provided practical help by giving further fields and the site in the town.

Most of those accused of killing are imprisoned in the Byumba area, some three hours drive away. The groups have provided money for their relatives to travel to visit them. As they visit, they have spread the good news of what is happening at home and have found that several of the prisoners have become believers.

Gacaca *and the community*
Many of the members of the groups have been elected as trusted members of the community to sit in the *Gacaca* courts. In January 2001 many prisoners were released, which was a real test for the unity of the groups. Those released came into three categories:

1 *Those who had no dossiers against them.* When they came home those who were genuinely innocent were usually received back and helped to face their anger at unjust imprisonment. Many had become believers in prison and now extended forgiveness to those who had accused them. Others were accused by members of the community in local courts, and if they did not accept their guilt were sent back to prison for full trial by *Gacaca* later.

2 *Those who admitted their guilt and had served eight years in prison.* Many of these have asked forgiveness of the families of those they had harmed, resulting in mutual acceptance in the community as they visit each other in their homes. Many testify as to how they became believers in prison and have joined the preaching group, telling how God forgives even murderers.

3 *The old and the sick or those who were under twelve years old when they were accused.* As above, these people have been received back and are helped as they have need.

Teaching
Originally MOUCECORE taught several seminars in the church, all of which were of immense help. The groups now choose two people to attend seminars in Kigali. When they return, they teach the others what they have learned. The most helpful seminars have been:

• Unity and reconciliation
• Healing inner wounds

- Learning how to pray and intercede
- Development and income-generating projects
- Helping to protect against HIV/AIDS and supporting those who have it. One great joy is that of the fifteen orphans who have been helped to get married, not one tested positive for HIV in a country where the national statistic amongst young people is about 13,9 per cent.[2] "This shows that they are putting into practice what we teach," said Emmanuel.

Jesus said, "Let your light so shine before men, that they may see your good works and glorify your Father in heaven" (Matthew 5:16). The light from Kiramuruzi has spread in all directions through the country. Many have come to see for themselves what is going on, from all Christian denominations, political parties and even from the Muslim community.

Where there was suspicion and division between denominations there is now unity; where the 63 original returning refugees had felt separated and alien, the 1,002 returnees are now totally integrated and considering themselves fully Rwandan; where widows and those whose husbands were imprisoned had regarded each other with suspicion and hatred, they have repented and asked each other for forgiveness.

Their prayer is that this light will continue to grow throughout the land and that it will be to God's glory. May God fully restore the years that the locusts have eaten.

Notes
1. Not her real name
2. UNAIDS statistics for 2003

Bibliography

History of Rwanda and the Genocide

Bilinda, Lesley, *The Colour of Darkness*, London, Hodder & Stoughton, 1996

Bilindabagabo, Alexis, *Rescued by Angels*, Lancaster PA, Acorn Press, 2001

Dallaire, Roméo, *Shake Hands with the Devil*, New York, Carroll and Graf, 2003

Gourevitch, Philip, *We Wish to Inform You That Tomorrow We Will Be Killed with Our Families*, London, Picador, 1999

Guillebaud, Meg, *Rwanda: The Land God Forgot?*, London, Monarch, 2002

Human Rights Watch, *Leave None to Tell the Story*, New York, 1999

Human Rights Watch/Africa, *Shattered Lives: Sexual Violence during the Rwandan Genocide and its Aftermath*, New York, 1996

Keane, Fergal, *Season of Blood: A Rwandan Journey*, London, Penguin, 1995

Melvern, L R, *A People Betrayed: The Role of the West in Rwanda's Genocide*, London, Zed, 2000

Prunier, Gerard, *The Rwanda Crisis: History of a Genocide*, London, C Hurst, 1995

Rutayisire, Antoine, *Faith under Fire*, Essex, African Enterprise, 1995

Forgiveness and Reconciliation

Arnold, Johann Christoph, *The Lost Art of Forgiving*, Farmington PA, The Plough Publishing House, 1998

—, *Why Forgive?*, Farmington PA, The Plough Publishing House, 2000

Arnott, John, *The Importance of Forgiveness*, Tonbridge, Sovereign World, 1997, 2003

Augsburger, David, *The Freedom of Forgiveness*, Chicago, Moody Press, 1988

Botman, H Russell and Petersen, Robin M (eds), *To Remember and to Heal: Theological and Psychological Reflections on Truth and Reconciliation*, Cape Town, Brommaert Press, 1996

Dante, Tori, *Our Little Secret: My Life in the Shadow of Abuse*, London, Hodder & Stoughton, 2001

Frost, Brian, *Struggling to Forgive: Nelson Mandela and South Africa's Search for Reconciliation*, London, HarperCollins, 1998

Graham, Jim, *Forgiveness*, Reading, Scripture Union, 1991

Haugen, Gary, *Good News About Injustice*, Leicester, IVP, 1999

Holloway, Richard, *On Forgiveness: How can we Forgive the Unforgivable?*, Edinburgh, Canongate Books, 2002

Kendall, R T, *Total Forgiveness*, London, Hodder & Stoughton, 2001

Lampman, Lisa Barnes (ed) et al, *God and the Victim: Theological Reflections on Evil, Victimization, Justice and Forgiveness*, Grand Rapids, Eerdmans, 1999

Lederach, John Paul, *Building Peace: Sustainable Reconciliation in Divided Societies*, Washington, United States Institute of Peace, 1997

—, *The Journey Toward Reconciliation*, Scottdale PA, Herald Press, 1999

Lloyd, Dr Rhiannon with Bresser, Kristine, *Healing the Wounds of Ethnic Conflict*, Geneva, Mercy Ministries, 2001

Lucado, Max, *He Chose the Nails*, Nashville, Word Publishing, 2000

Monbourquette, John, *How to Forgive: A Step-by-step Guide*, London, Darton Longman and Todd, 2000

Parker, Russell, *Healing Wounded History*, London, Darton Longman and Todd, 2001

Prince, Derek, *Atonement: Your Appointment with God*, Grand Rapids, Chosen Books, 2000

Sittser, Gerald, *A Grace Disguised: How the Soul Grows Through Loss*, Grand Rapids, Zondervan, 1995

Tutu, Desmond, *No Future without Forgiveness*, London, Random House, 2000

Wink, Walter, *When Powers Fall: Reconciliation in the Healing of Nations*, Minneapolis, Fortress Press, 1997

Other books quoted

Aitken, Jonathan, *Prayers for People under Pressure*, London, Continuum, 2005

Cassidy, Michael, *The Passing Summer*, London, Hodder & Stoughton, 1989

Chesterton, G K, *What's wrong with the World*, 1910

Lewis, C S, *A Grief Observed*, Bantam Doubleday Dell, 1976

Pope, Alexander, *An Essay on Criticism*, 1711

Quintilian, *Epistle 101 to Lucilius*

Seneca, *Dialogue*

Warren, Rick, *The purpose Driven Life*, Grand Rapids, Zondervan, 2002

The Church Mission Society (CMS) works in many countries in Africa, Asia and Eastern Europe, preaching the gospel and working alongside local churches. CMS began its work in Rwanda in 1922, through the Ruanda Mission. Since then the Lord has blessed the work and the Episcopal Church of Rwanda has grown and spread throughout the country.

CMS continues to work with the Episcopal Church of Rwanda, by sending mission personnel, supporting specific church programmes through grants and sponsoring students. We particularly work with the church in the areas of health care, training of church leaders, reconciliation work and projects to support those left widowed or orphaned by the genocide or by AIDS.

Further information about the continuing work of CMS in mid-Africa, and across the world, can be found at www.cms-uk.org, or by writing to: CMS, Partnership House, 157 Waterloo Road, London SE1 8UU.

"In this most needed book, Meg Guillebaud has opened for us the despair that followed genocide in Rwanda, the dilemma of meting out justice and the drama of reconciliation and restoration at the cross. While her stories are deeply personal, Meg points as well to the responsibilities of groups, nations and states. This moving narrative should draw all to repentance, showing the way to forgiveness and healing." — **David Rawson,** Ambassador of the United States (ret.); United States Ambassador to Rwanda, 1994–6

"Like diamonds set on black velvet Meg Guillebaud recounts brilliant living vignettes of compassion, forgiveness, reconciliation, spiritual reality and moral courage from the lives of those who went through the unspeakable horrors of the Rwandan genocide. If you are wondering if the Christian gospel is relevant in these days read this book and be convinced it is not only relevant — it is desperately needed." — **Stuart Briscoe,** minister at large, Elmbrook Church, Brookfield, Wisconsin

The Rev. Meg Guillebaud is a minister in Rwanda. The third generation of her family to serve there, she grew up in the country and lost many childhood friends in the genocide — a history vividly described in her first book *Rwanda: the Land God Forgot?*